Aust. Mitchell

1431

BRITAIN:
Beyond the Blue Horizon

Austin Mitchell

Bellew Publishing
London

First published in Great Britain in 1989 by
Bellew Publishing Company Limited
7 Southampton Place, London WC1A 2DR

Copyright © Austin Mitchell 1989

ISBN 0 947792 16 3

Printed and bound in Great Britain
by Richard Clay Ltd, Bungay, Suffolk

Contents

Acknowledgements

The thesis contained in this book has been widely discussed with local parties, and friends and colleagues within and without the Labour Party who would prefer to remain anonymous, except Bob Chapman who is in New Zealand. Neil Kinnock provided an unwanted, and unnecessary, sabbatical to write it, and as soon as he did so, Labour moved ahead in the polls. My family put up without me, though they are probably happier that way, and the Grimsby Labour Party put up with me. Lynn Pougher, Joyce Benton and Anne Tate tolerated my changes of mind and text and still produced a manuscript. Micky Chittenden translated it into English. Emma Scott, Anju Gupta, Tom Restrick and Shaun Stewart did the research, demonstrating the value of those researchers who Parliament has now decided to drive from the Fun Factory, a move designed to ease the strain on our inadequate facilities by banning the users. Ib Bellew pushed the book forward and Nancy Duin imposed the necessary discipline. Though all these friends made the book possible, invitations to lynchings should be addressed to me. Lastly, thanks to Linda. She supported me, cheered me and backed me through a fairly miserable fall.

AUSTIN MITCHELL
Grimsby, March 1989

Preface

The first ten years of Queen Margaret's reign looked better to those abroad than they felt to those who endured them. Foreigners have seen the decade as a triumph of will over some remarkably recalcitrant material, but back home, after a sticky start and policies bordering on the perverse, her long reign looks as much due to Labour's failures as to her own success. The prospect of another ten years is now as much a question of how the opposition evolves as of whether the Queen-Empress's rejuvenation can be prolonged indefinitely.

The alternative to petty-Poujadism, implemented by men who should know better and driven by a woman who does not, is a broad movement for change. Britain needs a people's politics, responding to the wishes of the mass of the nation rather than to the imperatives of a central, dominant will imposed through cumbersome monoliths. Before it is too late, we British should make one last effort to become what has always eluded us: a freer, more prosperous society, its standards rising with growth, rather than a herd of subjects, disciplined by deflation, divided by decline. There is still time to choose growth, disperse power among the people and move forward to a prosperous pluralist future, rather than back to the values, divisions and rigours of the Victorians. Provided we look to the future and the people, not to the past and to party myths.

The vision is populist rather than partisan. No one in the Labour Party seriously believes 1991 can be another 1945, and even another 1974 looks a remote possibility. This is why it is better to look to people and to a broad coalition for change rather than to a unilateral grab for government, at best clutching it with the fingertips, more likely missing it entirely. Power on such a basis would be a weapon too fragile for the job of turning Britain round.

Poor Britain: bamboozled, betrayed, fed on lies and deceit and never given clear-sighted leadership because its politicians have drifted with the tide and called it purpose. We alone have had no industrial miracle, and were slipping slowly downhill – until Margaret Thatcher changed that into a determined charge down a dead-end street.

Her real success has been the doling out of gratuitous advice to the world and thin gruel to the people. Labour, the instrument that has long borne so many hopes for the better society, now looks incapable of building it on its own: not quite a major, not quite ready for the strategies of a minor. The world has changed while we have weakened ourselves by trying to revert back to what we can never be again. Our catching up has to be massive and urgent, embracing new strategies to goals that remain the same, narrowing our aim to what we can get rather than what we want. Labour must lead a national effort rather than working on its own, risking Britain's subjection to another decade of vainglorious futility as time and oil slip away.

Idealism encourages illusions and delusions of the type Labour flesh is heir to, but now an objective assessment of reality is of more use than all the party rhetoric we can muster. Accepting the reality of our situation can lead to hope for Labour and for Britain, for the failure of one means the failure of the other. Springtime is beginning for Labour, rather like 1961–4 revisited, and more than welcome after the long bitter winter of our discontent. It will replace futility with a sense of purpose. Yet it neither changes the fundamentals, nor obviates the case for new approaches.

The views argued here are partial and fallible, but it would be trivial to dismiss them as disloyal. I first joined Labour in 1956 and it is not exactly career-enhancing to argue for sense, particularly if one turns out to be right, the supreme disqualification for any politician. It is much safer to be wrong on the scale of 1979–82. Frustrating as ten years under the steamroller have been, they could be counted as necessary learning processes were Labour still the simple effective instrument for change it once was. If it is not, and especially as time is getting short, we must look to alternative strategies and blame those whose follies or compliance undermined Labour's ability to fulfil its essential purposes on its own.

The politics of party cooperation are neither as simple nor as clear-cut as the Yah Boo fun of two-party competition, but the former may be all that remains available. Nor are they left or right, though it is odd to be suddenly on the left of the party, as the fragmenting Left of the early 1980s scurry behind. Surviving Gaitskellites now defend such dangerously radical courses as withdrawal from the European Community, low defence spending, planning, public enterprise, cooperation and equality as the former advocates of a siege economy (RIP) embrace the EC, and those of the dirigistic state clutch proportional representation and decentralization to their breasts. Consistency, too, is a political disadvantage, but at least the party should learn that fashionable fads and chanted slogans now offer less than realism, which requires us to mobilize every dynamic force against a government that blocks the path to betterment and every prospect for Britain. In a society where parties have not delivered and are not acclaimed, and where people are withdrawing from politics, Labour must seek a new *modus operandi*, and adjust to a new world.

1
The Deadlocked Democracy

Careful nurture and total fulfilment have ensured that the varicose ardours of the nymph at 60-plus are even greater than those of the nymph at 50. They do not bring wisdom nor any willingness to admit error, but despite this, Margaret Thatcher is more confident, more regal and ever more ready with sermons and unerringly over-simplified answers. Yet the ten-year Outward Bound course she has inflicted on Britain has failed. Her undertaking was to regenerate through strict economic morality and the market. The pain lingers. All hope is gone. Thatcherism can be written off as a ten-year march down a dead-end street, just another in the long line of busted flushes thrown up by Britain's long decline and the 'toil of dropping buckets into empty wells and growing old in drawing nothing up'. Each attempted to reverse comparative decline. Most ended by wasting the nation's time, and compounding its problems – and none more so than Thatcherism.

The decade with the greatest potential is ending with minimal achievement. Loud claims that Thatcherism has saved the nation will go on, fiddled figures will pour out to persuade us to ignore the evidence of our own senses. Government and its backing group – the Great British Reassurance Machine of the media – have invested too much in Thatcherism to admit that it was all a futile mistake. Those who see politics as the art of the plausible come to believe their own propaganda. The more the facts contradict it, the more they will fiddle the figures, use advertising to con the people at the people's own expense and bully the bearers of bad news.

Yet they have no idea what to do. The strategies have failed. Only those alternatives that Margaret has already ruled out are now on offer. As the Lawson 'boomlet' splutters out, a miraclette with an exceedingly short shelf-life is being seen as unsustainable, having plunged the country into an overseas deficit as big as the Americans', and every inhabitant into debt.

Comparative decline has been postponed for but a few short years. Now, with deflation, it resumes: a sad slide to national failure. The Thatcher solution was different to its predecessors: Maudling growth, Wilsonian white heat, Barber boom, Callaghan corporate endeavour. It promised more and did so more confidently, but it also inflicted more damage and ended by wasting the greatest opportunity to expand ever offered to any nation: OIL. The gift God placed in the North Sea to prove He was not a Muslim has financed moralizing irresponsibility. The foreign exchange benefits that have come from oil have resulted in the importation of manufactured goods to the destruction of jobs in Britain; its tax revenues have supported the unemployed thus created; its capital flows have been invested in the productive capacity of competitors. Oil could have reversed the slide. Instead, the bulk of it has been wasted to keep a minority government in power.

So a Thatcher decade, which began with a massive and unnecessary deflation, ends with another, bringing the country full circle, with nothing done to rebuild our shabby, run-down society or to invest in our future. The industrial base of nationhood is unable to pay its way in the world, to provide jobs or a tolerable standard of living. Britain is unable to afford the standards of an advanced industrial society and is ceasing to be one.

With oil self-sufficiency ending within a third of a decade, and oil output falling away steadily after 1995, we are drifting nearer a disaster that has been looming for a quarter of a century. How do we survive, pay our way and support our standard of living with a shrunken, uncompetitive manufacturing base, a population that is under-skilled, under-trained and under-educated? Particularly when we have compounded the problem by weakening industry to a degree that no competitor ever did, saying we were making it leaner and fitter while it was merely becoming anorexic.

A government that enthrones the market cannot opt out when markets work against Britain, as they must in decline. A government that sought salvation in deregulation and internationalization will not reverse either when they harm. If its highest wisdom is pulling out of management and refusing intervention, responsibility, protection or prescription, it cannot resume any of these when all become necessary. Change of policy requires change of government. The problem is economic, but the prior difficulty is political – the deadlocked democracy.

This government has used the oil to dig itself in, and as it has done so, the stresses that test democratic parties focused on a stymied, frustrated opposition, which has compounded them and buckled under the strain. Britain's party and electoral systems are both out of adjustment with the social base, so the levers of change have rusted. The swing of the pendulum has given way to the dictatorship of the minority. No longer a Mother of Parliaments, but a rubber stamp in the hands of the Prime Minister. No longer a cabinet and party restraining and guiding, but Maggie's minions. No longer a sensitive democracy but an elective dictatorship. The machinery of democracy has become a steamroller driven ever more maniacally by a government that has lost its way. Opposition is condemned to heckle the steamroller as it drives over them and anything else in its way.

The only British safeguard against a strong executive used to be the fact that it could be readily ejected. Now the Dictatorette cannot be. In the past, change came from the democratic revolution – throwing out the government as public opinion and the national mood changed, and as the reaction against governmental failure built up, producing a new mood. This was given coherence and leadership by the opposition, which put forward its agenda for change, and came to power to implement it as the swing cost the government votes and seats. The machinery of change was the two-party system, – its agency the electoral system, amplifying the swing to give any incoming government the power to carry through its programme.

Other countries have changed governing parties in the 1980s: the United States from Carter to Reagan, France from the long dominant Right to socialism, then cohabitation, then back to semi-socialism; West Germany from SPD to CDU. In Britain, Mrs Thatcher goes on (and on). The machinery of change is jammed, despite failures that would have had most previous governments out on their ears. Mass unemployment, poverty on a scale unknown since the 1930s, redundancies and closures – all are taken for granted. The worst deflation and the highest interest rates since the war, the impoverishment and deliberate rundown of the welfare state have not generated a mood for change. Opposition is divided, devoting time and effort to internal bickering and policy processes that involve belatedly catching up with a hypnotic government by plumping for the integration of markets, showing itself more communitaire than government, and toning down its demands rather than warning the nation of the problems to come. It plays safe by urging caution, respectability, discipline and generally presenting itself as the medicine of the economy to a nation that is already over prescribed. Selling policies relevant to the stringencies of the 1990s to an electorate lulled by the false affluence of the 1980s is an impossible task, but Labour has been too busy catching up with the present to think about the future.

So a failed government is enthroned, the dictatorship of the minority fastened on the country. Unless there is an unheralded disaster, or it develops a sudden penchant for *felo de se* – a change of mood occasionally seen before but as yet not experienced in the mid-Parliament torpids – the failed government looks impregnable. Opposition politicians pray for either or both of these, but that is the extent of their influence.

Britain drifts. The rest of the world gets richer. On the bridge, the Captain exudes confidence and energy, clicking balls as frenetically as Captain Queeg, and with even more painful consequences for the other officers, most of whom have few enough to spare. The officers are doubtful, but about the Captain rather than the course; with eyes down, they are more anxious about their own prospects of succession than the ship's survival. The crew serve dutifully, subdued by their incomprehending stupidity or their own desire to be promoted to the bridge. The passengers either gather rosebuds from a diminishing supply, or are kept down on the lower decks, well entertained if increasingly less well provided for. There are no signs of mutiny in them, but every symptom of a fading interest in the ship, its course and anything but their own cabins. HMS *Great Britain,* like USS *Caine,* can neither change course nor prepare for the colder, more dangerous waters that lie ahead. It has been left behind by the main convoy, limping, clanking, drifting in circles into irrelevance.

The policies to set the ship on a fruitful course are not difficult to devise. They have been applied by other countries to develop powerful economies; some have been used in Reagan's America. They still work. Britain needs them desperately. Yet they are only relevant to a nation-state, which Britain is ceasing to be. They require political change, which is unlikely. So the odds are that the arguments for an alternative will go unheard. A 40 per cent government will be left to preside, unperturbed and imperturbable, over a half-cock economy, providing inadequately for a three-quarter society, all the while drifting towards disaster . . .

. . . And by default. The default is mainly Labour's. It can save the nation, but first it must defeat the government. That requires a coalition for change broad enough to win a majority. Instead it has shrunk, failing to be a successful social democratic party of the European type, because it allowed its working-class base to be destroyed and has not delivered the goods, failing, too, to take the alternative route by becoming looser, more permeable, even a polycentric party like the American Democrats. The decline of industry has weakened the base of social democracy, but liberal democracy is more saleable. Labour must straddle two markets and must do so as the price, not of victory, but of survival. Nothing in politics is inevitable, not even Margaret Thatcher; she only seems immortal because she appears to go on eternally. Yet the balance of probabilities is that Conservatives will remain in government, coping with complex economic problems at the intellectual level of 'Disgruntled of Grantham' and enforcing prejudice with the hurtling handbag. They do not have to win the next election. Even losing they could stay in power, and all their skill in the politics of duplicity will be applied to that end. Economic well-being will not help them as much as it did in 1987, but then it put them far enough ahead to survive with ease (and seats to spare) the political consequences of, at least, a soft economic landing, and possibly a hard one.

There are ways of undermining the hegemony if Labour dare espouse them. Although the government is likely to win, it can be helped to lose. Labour cannot reach power on its own but can use stilts. A full programme of socialist change is impossible, but the tiller can be turned. Yet even that minimalist prospectus requires major changes in Labour's attitudes and approaches if it is to succeed in the new politics of a consumer democracy. The change requires transformation. However, merely trudging back from the brink of Labour's own DIY disaster has been a difficult and slow process.

Parties have to transform themselves while retaining their relevance by remaining the same. The Conservatives do it well and often by killing the king. Labour is more naïve (a.k.a. principled) and too arthritic, and vested interests are too deeply entrenched. It finds political conjuring tricks difficult, although it can do them when desperate. The changes cannot even be justified by the only argument parties heed: that if they are to deliver success, or simply remain viable, changes must be made. Yet changes do improve the prospect, and it is better to make change a springboard to opportunity than a consequence of defeat, as would happen if Labour were to face an election as is. If nothing is done before 1992, that would mean that a failed government would sit on, as Britain goes five years further down the road of decline, with five years more of irreversible Thatcherism, while Labour's problems – the threat to its Scottish base, the tilting of the population to the Tory South, the drain of ability and the taint of inexperience – become five years worse. The answer is to change Labour into a broader-based people's party, in communion with the nation, prepared to work with others, a broad expression of the country's wishes rather than the agent of a dying class. Not exactly what socialists want: supporting Labour is about building a better world. Yet the best way to repair the damage and the key to several futures. To Labour's own. To ending the government's tenure (without a broad, viable alternative, it is enthroned). To Britain's, too. Unless the political deadlock is broken, we cannot glimpse the brand new day. As perennial optimists, we socialists believe it will dawn beyond the all-too-blue horizon. Yet as realists, we must chart new routes to the hills for a glimpse of it.

2
Malice in Blunderland

Britain is the limping failure of the advanced industrial world. Other Western (and not so Western) countries have experienced 'economic miracles' powering to industrial strength. Britain has made the slow crawl backwards. At the start of the post-war period, it was well ahead of most of the world: a powerful industrial machine largely intact, substantially modernized, well invested during the 1930s and the war, running at full power. It supported one of the world's highest standards of living, and that was more fairly shared than most, particularly as the pioneer welfare state was built to reward the people for their efforts. A quarter of the world's manufactured trade was British, sustained by close ties with captive markets, carried by a huge British-built, and owned, merchant fleet, financed by British financial services through the City of London.

From there, it was downhill all the way. Other economies grew, invested, improved productivity, training, research, design. Economies of scale spread the cost of improvements over a larger output as British industry never could, so that the industries of others reached a virtuous cycle of self-sustaining, export-led growth and, with it, the ability to price to markets and win them. Britain grew slowly, by STOP–GO lurches, dependent on the domestic market, not exports. Anyone who took risks to expand in the GO phases was subsequently penalized by rises in interest rates, cuts in demand. Profits were too low to finance adequate investment, training, research and design. Economies of scale escaped us: the problem was simply keeping production going. Britain's was a 'make do and mend' economy. Low aspirations were inbred.

In a competitive world, differences compound. Growth begets investment, which begets growth and productivity, which is, in the main, a feature of greater output leading to further growth. Decline compounds to more decline as industry becomes less competitive, loses heart and investment. Economies that grow become more powerful. Economies that do not fall behind and become vulnerable. Industries that fail to compete are picked off by more powerful competitors. Britain lost motorbikes, then cars, machine tools, office equipment and, more recently, computers and information technology. Great names, and major exporters, went under or became façades for imports. As imports gained an increasing share of the home market, the traditional base of domestic industry was gnawed away. It had no firm ground to sustain it. Demand could not be expanded because it fuelled competing economies, not ours, sucking in more and more imports: the Keynesian multiplier went to live in West Germany.

Everytime the British economy expanded, it ran into balance-of-payments problems. That ceiling was never raised. Each balance-of-payments problem became more serious, and the deflation to cope with it became harder, reining back demand by hitting the engine of growth – manufacturing – through high interest rates and an overvalued exchange, both damaging long-term prospects to 'save' the short term. The industrial economy was losing power, unable to pull its load, or provide the goods to which a nation far better at consumption (and distribution and advertising) than production was becoming addicted.

To maintain public spending and benefits at a halfway decent level, taxation had to provide what growth did not. It became an angry issue. Public provision and the standard of living both grew more slowly, becoming shabbier as the gap between us and everyone else widened. Investment, research, design, the infrastructure that serves industry, training, management, education, the networks of suppliers and services, new technologies – all were less than adequate. Without the same kinds of profits as its competitors, industry did not invest, train, or improve its products, falling further behind and becoming obsessed with self-protection against takeovers and with defensive strategies.

*

Labour was twice brought to office to deal with this. In the 1960s, it failed, and in the 1970s, it struggled to contain the crisis and keep the rickety machine going. Its disciplines produced revolt, its strategies inflicted pain and discredited its ultimate objectives because they were assumed to be part of it. The electorate resented cuts in living standards and real pay. Unions revolted in the winter of discontent, attempting to make up by industrial action what growth was failing to provide. Labour, the party of duty, reduced to cleaning up Tory messes, broke under the strain and committed suicide – just as the polls were indicating that the electorate was beginning to learn the lessons of failure and accept reality.

So, in 1979, Margaret Thatcher entered her reign with a new, and simple, strategy for saving the nation by doing the opposite to Labour, thus throwing away gains, goodwill and all the painful learning processes, but giving the Tory Party the only definition of itself with which it has ever been comfortable: that it is against what Labour is for. Mrs Thatcher decided to enthuse her party rather than unnerve it as Ted Heath had done. He has his supporters still (very still, most of them), but his legacy, and that of post-war politics, was thrown overboard. Thatcherite policies were applied with the absolute certainty of the second-rate mind. Britain began its last and most drastic attempt to reverse the decline. This new beginning was inaugurated with more confidence, trumpeted with louder and more lavish public relations exercises than any predecessor. There was no alternative.

From out of the blue, Thatcherism was sold to the nation as a solution to decline. Yet it was really a product of it: part of that search for answers that decline precipitates. The extremism of Thatcherism indicates that it was a late throw in the end-game, following a long series of other failures: 'Bonfire of Controls', National Plan, Selsdonism, EEC membership, social contract. Thatchernomics was superficially the easiest – virtue is simple – but in practice, it turned out to be the harshest, a Final Solution born of the gathering crisis, brought to power and given credibility by it. A consequence of decline posing as the answer.

Being a moralist and not an economist, Margaret Thatcher had the simple answers that carry credibility with an electorate as badly informed about the realities of industry and economics as its new leader. 'Set the people free,' provide incentives, manage the money supply on moral lines to produce 'sound money', roll back the state, cut taxes and all would be well. The implicit, but unstated, commitment was to cut the nation's coat to suit its shrunken cloth, but the nation was not told that, still less that vicuña coats would be enlarged, donkey jackets trimmed.

The programmes themselves did not win power; Labour threw it at the Tories. When the policies began to make things far worse, the nation might have accepted it, being conditioned to seeing suffering as an essential prelude to success. However, the people might equally have thrown out the Tories as they had done previous failures. Instead, Labour deprived them of the opportunity by depriving them of an alternative, and her messianic prejudices gave the Prime Minister the confidence to persevere through all the damage. Things would work because she was right. Follow the path of virtue and you will be OK. The nation plodded behind. It could do nothing else.

Britain could be great again, unemployment would fall, Britain would work, industry and the economy would regenerate – all that was needed was only the will to see the medicine through. As a consummate amateur actress – the St Joan of economics – Margaret Thatcher meant her every line. Yet at a ten-year distance, Thatcherism looks less like a coherent philosophy than successive improvisations centred on the impulses and instincts of its central driving force. As a politician, and the prey of events, Margaret Thatcher could hardly be wholly consistent. So she fought inflation while increasing public-sector prices; cut taxes while increasing the tax burden, the tax proportion of GDP (from 34 per cent in 1978–9 to 38 per cent in 1987–8) and indirect taxes; supposedly cut expenditure but actually increased it to pay for unemployment and poverty; spent more on the National Health Service while allowing it to deteriorate; 'set the people free' while crippling them with unemployment and high interest rates; let 1000 capitalists blossom while making more bankrupt – all the while claiming to govern less while doing more, centralizing more, interfering more.

The Prime Minister is a mistress of management by metaphor, like President Reagan. Her fundamental propositions have been the same as his. Despite the claim that they have been consistently applied, the government has, in fact, gone through three distinct phases and is now becoming bogged down in a fourth, depressingly similar to the first. That was the great deflation – Light Brigade economics – leading to an economic disaster but a PR triumph appealing to the Dunkirk spirit (one coat covers any mess) and the masochistic instincts of the British people, and making everything subsequent look good. Then came the slow recovery, of the type enjoyed by lunatics who stop beating heads against walls to discover how much better life is. Third, an expansion was announced as the fruits of success, but it really sprang from the reversal of basic policies on money supply and exchange rates. Finally, full circle, we are back to STOP, stuck in the Crippsian corset.

Labour had grappled with the worst economic crisis since the war by using high public spending to keep up demand, fair sacrifices and better benefits to protect the vulnerable, collective effort to defeat inflation by an incomes policy, and state help to faltering capitalism. The Tories seized on their opposites. Not more state to protect and manage but less. Not more taxation to support spending but less. Not cooperation against inflation but the market. There has never been such a total rejection of incumbent strategies and, thereby, of all the major elements of policy since the war.

The difficulties of the 1970s gave credence to the policies of the 1920s. Provide incentives on the grounds that the rich are not working hard enough because they do not have enough money. On the other hand, the poor, being different, are not working hard enough because they have too much: benefits are too high to make them work; the unions are resisting the natural desire of workers to take wage cuts to compete with the Japanese. So take the money from the poor and give it to the rich, and all will be well. Government's role is to let the market work, restricting its own intervention to controlling the money supply on the strictly monetarist lines imported into Britain, at about the same time as Dutch Elm disease, by Peter Jay and Samuel Brittan. No incomes policies, regional policies, planning, intervention, job schemes or support for lame ducks. Nothing but sound money secured by controlling the money supply and cutting the public-sector borrowing requirement.

Thatcherites believed in the quantity theory of money – more devalues – a belief that comes naturally to those who own much of it and are not keen to share. Brilliantly simple; disastrously wrong. Allowed to keep more of their 'own' money by a reduction of their social rent, business executives spent more time on the golf course, more money on imports, and got greedy.

Incentives hardly trickled down to the one group for whom they might have worked: the skilled who were in short supply, but had fewer jobs available. Rationally, it was more likely that high taxes would make people work harder in order to sustain a standard of living that would otherwise have fallen, than that the cutting of taxes, already with a low starting point, would stimulate effort.

The money supply thesis was even weaker. The supply could not be controlled without control of the banks, only rationed by high interest rates. Yet that meant a rise in the pound, which was already being pushed up by oil revenues. So economic strategy compounded a problem that was already becoming serious. Logically, oil required the pound to be kept down to encourage industry. Oil revenues do not provide jobs, and if allowed to push the exchange rate up, they destroy them. They were allowed. It did rise – to record levels and a peak in the second quarter of 1981, pioneering a disaster that the United States was later to follow. Export costs rose, pricing our goods out of foreign markets. Imports came pouring in, taking ever bigger shares of the British market. Profits evaporated. Firms closed, or threw overboard research, design, development, training and investment to stay afloat.

The four years from 1979 to 1982 were the greatest disaster in British economic history. A fifth of manufacturing capacity closed; 28 per cent of manufacturing jobs went. The workshop of the world became a net manufacturing importer. It could have been deliberate. Unemployment was the only way that many government intentions could be fulfilled: inflation came down from the heights to which the government had put it by doubling VAT; the power of the labour force was broken. Yet the scale of the disaster has subsequently taken on the appearance of an accident, half-understood consequences of a half-baked policy that got out of control. The incoming Tories had no idea how industry worked. They did not see it as the complex organism it is, fragile and readily damaged by hostile climatic charges, but as a simple mechanism responding to disciplines, sermons, morality.

Neither explanation – a deliberate policy or an accident – reflects credit on the government, but deciding between them is jesuitical. The consummation of high unemployment itself was devoutly wished. It was like using a guillotine to cure dandruff, but it yielded the effects that the government both wanted and took credit for. As a result, Margaret Thatcher was the first prime minister to see unemployment as a solution, not a problem. She derived so much benefit from it that any argument over whether the 2 million smoking P45s were in her hand accidentally or by design is useless. Coming in later with the same policies, Reagan eventually bent to reality and abandoned them, even as he continued to sing their praises. The American system is open and sensitive, and presidents must walk a tightrope, not drive a steamroller. There, howls of pain are heard and politics triumph. Here, the will of the elected dictatorship triumphs and it is enforced with the unerring certainty of a sleep walker.

The Tory Party was pathetically grateful. Margaret Thatcher had taken it back to power only five years after disaster. She stood head and shoulders above the party because they were on their knees. Having limited brain power themselves, they accepted the certainties of the second-class mind as genius. They are, in any case, a governing machine programmed to the instincts of a public school fag (which so many of them have been). Because, in our system of government, the executive controls the legislature by party, Margaret Thatcher could get away with murder. She did, and protest beyond the walls of the House of Commons was minimal. Industry – and particularly a CBI that is neither an effective confederation nor British, and does not represent industry either – accepted everything out of loyalty to the Tory Party and desire for tax cuts. Greater love hath no man than that he lay down his firm for his prejudices. From 1982, Reagan began changing the policies. Mrs Thatcher persevered, intoxicated by the damage.

She would have gone on longer, announcing that it was better to be tough than to be kind, and relying on the passivity of a nation which always feels virtuous when it is being punished, the supine prejudice of the CBI and the complacency of the Conservative Party to see her through. However, wiser counsels came from Professor Alan Walters, who pointed out that strategies designed to curtail the money supply were actually increasing it. High interest rates brought money flooding in to put up the pound and to increase the money supply, while the effect on production forced companies to borrow to meet their mounting interest bills, even to survive. Government was driving the economy downhill and interest rates ever upward: 17 per cent at the peak. Professor Walter's answer was to expand domestic credit, and overfund by borrowing more than needed while feeding the money back out to industry, thus bringing down the money supply figures and soaking up credit at the tax payers' expense. The pound fell as the monetarist ratchet was covertly eased.

The economy picked up, beginning the second phase of spluttering recovery from 1982–5. It was inadequate because the pound remained high, as did interest rates, but both were down from the heights, permitting some revival. Productivity increased because old capacity had been closed down to concentrate production in new, better-invested plants, much as a cricket team might put up its batting average by shooting the last four batsmen. Industry revived as the home market recovered, stimulated by the expansion of credit and the rise in house prices in the South-east, which, in turn, justified more credit in a North Sea bubble stimulated by the continuous creation of collateral. Exports improved because the Americans, having abandoned monetarism, had the biggest Keynesian deficit in history, stimulating a boom that, with the dollar reaching ludicrous heights in 1985, sucked in imports and raised the US share of UK exports of manufactures from 10.4 per cent in 1979 to 17.4 per cent in 1987. Two-thirds of the increase in British manufactured exports after 1979 went to the American market. All this was an improvement on what had gone before. Mean and marginal, but still recovery.

The contraction of industry and the rise of oil earnings, reaching a peak in 1986, made sterling a petro-currency. Then, in 1986, the oil price fell. Sterling came down with it. In the 1983 election, the Labour Party had suggested a devaluation of 30 per cent. Government spokesmen of the time had ridiculed this as a recipe for disaster. Now the pound came down by almost that figure with results so beneficial that the government, having done its best to stop the fall by maintaining high interest rates, took the credit, as if the recovery it produced was the logical result of their own policies rather than of their negation.

The expansion of the domestic economy was further stimulated by a credit explosion that amounted to a form of privatized Keynesian economics, with deficit financing by the private sector rather than the government. In combination with the falling pound, this produced a dramatic upswing. Exports picked up, imports were checked, expansion began. The government had accidentally discovered the secret of success: growth begets growth, improvement begets improvement. As production rose, productivity, a factor of production, improved. Increasing output brought unit costs down and held labour costs. Industry began to invest. Not quite the virtuous cycle, but a new experience for Britain, and one that achieved economic growth at rates of 5 and 6 per cent. Higher than our competitors'. Good enough for an election victory in 1987.

The boom was small compared to the needs of the economy. A higher and more sustained rate of growth was necessary to bring unemployment down and rebuild the economy. Britain's was heavily directed towards consumption, not investment. Because of the previous contraction and closures, too much of the demand was fed by imports, leading inevitably to a balance-of-payments problem. It was not enough to push total output back to 1979 levels. Unemployment fell only slowly, and what reduction there was was due more to job schemes, to low-paid jobs for women and to casual part-time work rather than to Mrs Thatcher's 'real' jobs.

It was like rain on a parched plain, but it needed to be boosted and sustained. Tragically, growth was not as high on the government's list of priorities as it was on the nation's list of needs. The government's priority was sound money, their enemy not unemployment but inflation, their aspiration not a British economic miracle but an orderly economy. So with the election out of the way, the Conservatives began to roll up their unintended boom, knowing that they would not be needing it for at least another three years. Nigel Lawson set about killing the goose that had laid his golden eggs by putting up interest rates early on. Then, after a brief period of reduced rates to cope with the stock market crash of October 1987, he increased them dramatically in 1988 with eight rises in three months. The second Thatcher deflation had begun. To balance trade, it would have to be massive and sustained.

The Americans had adjusted to a balance-of-payments problem that, on 1987 figures, was somewhat smaller in relation to GDP than Britain's in mid-to-late 1988. They did this by bringing the dollar down substantially to encourage exports and penalize imports. Britain adopted the opposite solution. The pound rose 20 per cent against the Deutschmark from DM 2.75 to DM 3.25, but much more in real terms. The government opted for dearer money and paying foreigners high interest rates to bring money in to close the gap. The US had kept domestic activity running at a growth rate of 4 per cent by transferring the weight from demand to manufacturing, including for export. Britain damped down demand and penalized manufacturing. The US had gone for survival by the real economy. Britain opted for the money economy. The Lawson miraclette was over – just another burst of unsustainable growth in the series of bursting bubbles that have occurred since the war, the main difference being that this government has had to burst its own. Britain was sentenced to two years hard. The consumer boom spluttered. The deflation that was required was as big as that from 1979 to 1981. Industry began to batten down the hatches. Nigel Lawson may continue to fiddle while Maggie burns, the last resort of the gambler and the prophet, but it is all over bar the boasting. What has been achieved by ten years of Thatcherism?

Mrs Thatcher is hardly modest in her own assessment. She

claims that Britain has been transformed, surging with initiative and enterprise, industry regenerated, unemployment falling, a nation holding its head high – 'things will never be the same again.' Halting the escalation of government spending, rolling back the powerful state, cutting taxation, enthroning sound money and balancing the budget have ended a 40-year misery. Decline is over, thanks to the first post-war prime minister to enshrine dogma and stick to it through thick and thin. No more betrayals, reversals or compromises; just right principles, single-minded will and a voice that, within a decade, deepened by almost an octave with the strain of preaching.

Commentators and pundits usually echo Margaret Thatcher's interpretation of herself. Yet her picture of Britain today is painted in moral terms, describing changes of mood and attitudes. Where there are figures, they are either fiddled or not quite up to the claims. Industrial output did expand, eventually, but not to the same degree as that of major competitors. Total taxation is up, and is still above 1979 levels as a proportion of GNP. The tax burden has been shifted, but the average family still pays a higher proportion of its income to the state and the average earner exactly the same proportion in direct taxes. More businesses are being formed, but more going bust. Exports are up but only by a third, compared to a doubling of imports. Finance is flourishing, manufacturing opting out, the pound high, interest rates higher to keep it there. Entrepreneurs are getting more, and paying themselves a lot more, but poverty is worse than ever, and the gap between the two is greater.

Comment is free but facts are manipulatable. The real key to Margaret Thatcher's success is good publicity, and better luck: she had an incompetent opposition; and she enjoyed a benefit both parties had struggled for – oil. These two factors combined to give her her one real success: breaking the pattern of governments coming in, grappling with a problem and being booted out – a pattern that had characterized British politics since 1964. Thatcher's triumph is political, its manifestation three election victories in a row. However, in the face of enormous opportunity, her economic achievement is minimal.

The government claims success because inflation is down

from the levels to which it had itself put it up in 1979–80. In making inflation the test, it does no more than Labour: dodging real assessment by concentrating on irrelevancies. Inflation is not the problem but a symptom of a nation where too much wealth is in too few hands, producing envy and pressures, and of an economy that cannot produce enough to satisfy demand. The Tories saw inflation as too much money pursuing too few goods, but if that is so, the solution is more goods, not less money, for to cut that damages demand. Any fool can bring down inflation by killing jobs, and Margaret Thatcher certainly achieved that, but she has not been able to manage the real trick of genuinely defeating it by expanding production in conditions of high growth, full employment and stable prices which lower unit costs and greater efficiency allow. Here was the trick by which every competitor pulled in growth phases that we have never enjoyed. It still eludes Britain.

The most basic test of failure is the level of unemployment: 2,000,000 on the government's much-cooked figures, which show only those claiming (and entitled to) benefit, rather than, as the International Labour Office recommends, those actually out of work. Even that figure is still 1 million over the figure at the start of Conservative rule, and 1 million less than the more realistic measure of those out of work and seeking employment. The official unemployment rate is 8 per cent compared with 5 per cent in the United States – an average for the period 1980 to 1987 of 10.3 per cent compared with an OECD average for the same period of 7.1 per cent. During these crucial years, few other OECD countries had a higher average rate than Britain. None has lost jobs on the scale of a Conservative government that is still, in 1989, 1 million jobs down on the total it inherited – the first government to have fewer jobs than it started with.

Productivity increased by 2.1 per cent per annum averaged over the period 1979–87. This was lower than Japan's productivity rate but better than any other competitor's, better than the OECD average of 1.4 per cent, and better than the British performance from 1973–9 of 1.2 per cent, which was itself slightly lower, though only by 0.2 per cent, than the then OECD average. Yet the difference is marginal and the rate of improvement lower than the 3.0 per cent achieved from 1963

Comparative Performance Indicators (OECD)

	GDP (1980 prices) Average annual rate of growth			Labour productivity Average annual rate of growth			Unemployment rate Average		
	1968–73	1973–79	1979–87	1968–73	1973–79	1979–87	1968–73	1974–79	1980–87
UK	3.2	1.4	1.9	3.0	1.2	2.1	2.5	4.2	10.3
US	3.0	2.6	2.3	0.7	0.0	0.6	4.7	6.8	7.7
Japan	8.4	3.6	3.9	7.3	2.9	2.9	1.2	1.9	2.5
W. Germany	4.9	2.3	1.5	4.1	2.9	1.5	0.8	3.5	6.9
France	6.2	2.8	1.7	5.0	2.5	1.8	2.6	4.7	9.0
Italy	4.6	2.6	2.3	4.6	1.8	1.7	5.4	6.2	9.1
Canada	5.4	4.2	2.8	2.4	1.3	1.0	5.4	7.2	9.8
Average	4.3	2.7	2.4	2.9	1.4	1.4	3.2	5.0	7.1

to 1973, which had been higher than the OECD average of 2.9 per cent. The increase is difficult to attribute to the new realism. The early improvement was due to closures, the later to the expansion after 1985. Over the whole period, the old, labour-intensive industries with inflexible job demarcation gave way to more rational allocations, all of which improved matters. None of this brought Britain to the level of its competitors. In 1986, British productivity was 30 per cent less than in the US and 25 per cent less than in Europe. That gap will take decades to close.

Britain's economic 'miracle' is a Milan Shroud. Wealth creation depends on the total numbers available to create it, as well as the productivity of those in work. Here there was no increase in productivity up to 1985. Since then, it has been minimal.

The growth that Britain needed to catch up was not generated – in fact, several years of compounding were lost. The average of 1.9 per cent per annum is lower than the OECD's average of 2.4 per cent and lower than the UK growth in the 1960s of 3.2 per cent. Even the underlying increase of 7 per cent in manufacturing output in the later part of 1988 was less than the increases of 8.1 per cent in 1960, 9.3 per cent in 1964,

7.7 per cent in 1968 and 9.3 per cent in 1973, and this despite the fact that the scope for increasing output is much greater when unemployment is so much higher. Taking the three years of the Lawson 'miracle', manufacturing output went up by 14 per cent during 1985–8 compared with 24 per cent from 1952 to 1955, 14 per cent from 1963 to 1966 and 12 per cent from 1966 to 1969, while during the nine years between 1979 and 1988, it went up by only 7 per cent, one-sixth the rate during the period 1963–9 when resources were much nearer full employment and inflation was only 3.5 per cent, compared with 7.5 per cent under this government.

High and sustained growth at over 5 per cent would have been necessary to bring down unemployment. It reached 4 per cent from 1986 to 1988 but proved unsustainable. Failure was concealed only because oil had removed the uncertainties of the 1970s, and the growth went disproportionately to those areas where it could buy the highest electoral returns. Nor was anything else possible. The real economy has been trapped by its growing dependence on finance. Money went into asset appreciation, particularly in houses, in property and, until October 1987, in shares, causing the overheating of the economy while still immune to the rise in interest rates that it produced, just as long as asset inflation outdistanced interest costs. Only industry was hit.

The high-interest-rate economy sucked money in from overseas, pushing the pound up, causing a deterioration in the balance of payments (the reverse of the capital account), and justifying, through hope of further appreciation, more inflows. The result was continuous overvaluation and an economy awash with money too dear to use for productive investment. As a result of the overvaluation, imports of finished manufactures in the third quarter of 1988 rose above the previous year's level by 20 per cent, 49 per cent up on 1985 and 139 per cent up on 1980. Exports were up by only 21 per cent on 1985 and 35 per cent on 1980. Imports of manufactures have increased four times faster than exports, so British industry is even less capable of coping with demand expansion than ten or twenty years ago. A horrendous trade gap was the result, a disaster not just due to the importing of consumer goods and cars, but to the fact that the whole economy was becoming addicted to imports at every level, from capital goods to components, even to part-finished goods for working up here. All were cheaper than local production. Britain was becoming a warehouse economy.

Industry could neither face the competition nor carry on its old role as the national provider. It rose to seize the opportunity that came with devaluation, but it had been too badly damaged to make the best of it. Imports had taken too tight a grip to be beaten back, and industry slipped into its old habits: growth by takeover and acquisitions; exploitation of existing markets rather than expansion; using profits to diversify rather than build. It was still defensive. After the way it had been treated, who can wonder? The future had not been built. It had been thrown away because industry had been gravely injured and was certain to be further harmed by the deflation resulting from the deficit.

In the US, Senator Daniel Moynihan said that President Reagan's economic achievement was to borrow trillions of dollars from the Japanese and throw a party. Mrs Thatcher took the wealth flowing from the North Sea and threw her own, but being more mean spirited, she invited only her friends. Ten million Americans got jobs, making everyone better off and Reagan the most popular of recent American presidents. He boosted the worker and was proud to have done so. Mrs Thatcher could not prevent her distaste showing through and gave workers lectures for wanting to earn more.

Oil was the main cause of whatever success the Thatcher government achieved. It generated tax revenues – £80 billion over the first nine years – so that taxation did not have to press as heavily on business or the economy. As a political issue, tax became less relevant and taxes themselves less oppressive, and the Conservative government could sing its own praises for pretending to cut them. Oil provided a balance-of-payments surplus since Britain no longer had to import energy and could afford a higher level of imports. It generated capital for the investment that British industry so desperately needed after years of low profits. Here was the chance to update and upgrade.

Thatcherites reply that oil is a marginal factor, adding only some 4 per cent to the GNP even at its height, yet the contribution from oil was crucial. The margin between success and failure in the British economy has always been narrow. Two or three percentage points on the growth rates, plus the ability to keep growth going through balance-of-payments constraints, would have transformed Britain. Our long failure has been comparative, our problems at the margin: lower growth, lower investment, the balance-of-payments constraint – all guaranteeing that every expansion produced a surge of imports, threatening payments and the pound. So each expansion was damped, eliminating the market for increased production. Oil raised that crucial ceiling. It could have permitted sustained expansion, growth compounding growth, with the oil used to ride out the balance-of-payments consequences as Britain had never been able to do before. The potential contribution was, therefore, enormous. That was what the government threw away to make oil an agent of destruction, obliterating large sections of manufacturing and millions of jobs by making the pound higher than it would otherwise have been.

This could have been offset by expansion, or by ekeing the oil out, as Norway has done. The Conservatives opted for deflation and high interest rates, pushing the pound up and so ruining industry. Investment and expansion needed cheap money. To survive, industry needed to export and to defeat imports in its home market. Both aims required a competitive exchange rate. Finance, on the other hand, benefited from high interest rates and wanted a high pound to sustain its own international operations and investments. Finance won. Industry was doubly punished and could only flourish when circumstances, such as the fall in the oil price in 1986, disturbed the plan by bringing the pound down. The rest of the time, industry was neither boosted nor treated with the care that unhealthy plants require. The fact that it did so well in improving productivity and output and, against all the odds, in holding prices and labour costs during that brief period of respite showed what it could do given the opportunity.

It could yet do so again. The Conservatives attached too little importance to industry. They looked for jobs to the service industries, for survival to finance. Yet in practice, industry is basic to jobs, growth, exports and imports and hence to the balance of payments. If a weakened industry leads to a balance-of-payments gap, finance cannot fill it. Even after foreign investors have been seduced by PR hype, enthused by ideology and preached to by the Prime Minister, they still have to take account of fundamentals. The balance of payments is the most crucial indicator of economic health because it measures the prospects of a fragile economy in a competitive world, dictating the level of jobs and industry by measuring a country's success at making things and selling them to the world. It is a ceiling to prospects. An economy that wastes oil and its opportunities, that lacks the powerful competitive industrial base of a West Germany or Japan, might seem even less attractive if it also undermines the internationally traded sector on which survival depends – particularly if the oil price falls, or the world turns nasty. An economy that discounts industry thus becomes the victim of the forces it installs in industry's place. Those who live by confidence can also die by it unless they have built a powerful, competing industrial base. The government had driven itself, and the nation, into a trap. By running the economy for money, not making and selling things, it weakened Britain's long-term prospects. The government could only sustain confidence by paying a higher and higher ransom in interest rates.

The nemesis of Thatcherism is the balance-of-payments disaster. Its symptoms emerged in 1981 when Britain became, for the first time, a net importer of manufactures. By 1986, this meant a small overall deficit, by 1987 a £2.5 billion deficit, and by 1988, a £14 billion deficit. Earlier equal to 3.1 per cent of GDP, it was 4.0 per cent on the July to November figures compared to the 3.7 per cent American deficit in 1987. By contrast, in 1970, we had had a surplus of 1.7 per cent of GDP. We have always had a favourable non-oil balance of trade, and have nearly always paid our way in the world, even when we had to import oil. Now we cannot.

This was a disastrous but inevitable consequence of government policies. Some of the failure was due to the closure of capacity that would have been profitable at a lower exchange rate. More was due to the boost in demand stimulated by easy credit and tax cuts, which went mainly to imports because British industry could not expand quickly enough. Yet the basic cause was the overvalued pound, its real value up 21 per cent between the fourth quarter of 1986 and the second of 1988. The proper response would have been to allow the market to operate, bringing down exchange rates as the US had done, thus putting up the price of imports, subsidizing exports and gradually redressing the balance. Markets were not to be allowed to operate in this crucial area. Britain was to have high interest rates, over double those of competitors, the exchange rate of the pound being increased to 'fight inflation'. The gap due to the high exchange rate was to be dealt with by putting it up even higher. A crisis generated by pricing exports out, imports in, was to be met by increasing the price of domestic manufactures in foreign-exchange terms and by making imports cheaper.

Monetarists such as Sam Brittan saw benefits in the deficit because it syphoned demand off to other countries, preventing an inflationary take-off here – a masochistic view that assumed that jobs exported were less important than nice readings on the dials in monetarism's theoretical lab. The government claimed to be unperturbed: Britain had invested overseas for the contingency. Yet these investments were private and not available to make up the deficit. Even if they could have been brought back, disinvestment on the 1988 scale would have eaten them in less than a decade. 'The deficit is a private sector matter,' said the Chancellor. Yet that made it a question of confidence. Money was coming in for investment purposes, but the bulk of it was short term, attracted by high interest rates. A short-term strategy was a risky one, given the confidence factor. A flight from sterling was increasingly possible.

Short-term finance is footloose. The money flowing round the world seeking a return has transformed national economies into casinos, influenced by mood, images, psychology, even herd instinct, and ever ready to jump, triggered by the continuous calculus of the trade-off between interest rates and exchange-rate prospects. With a government committed to deflation, sustained by high interest rates, both look good. So the Thatcher government, from the start, set out to keep interest rates high and make Britain attractive to money flows. It then proclaimed these as indications of the world's confidence in Britain and its government. In fact, flows create a self-fulfilling prophecy. Attracted by a rising currency, incoming money heightens the rise, which led to overshooting in both Britain and the United States in the 1980s. Noticeably this happens only in economies where finance is dominant, barriers low. Industrial countries manage their exchange rates more sensibly.

Rises cannot go on for ever. A point of calculus is reached. Then the money market assesses its gains from high interest rates against potential losses from an exchange-rate fall. This is the lemming limit: the possibility of a mass exodus producing an exchange-rate crisis, and ever-higher interest rates to stop the rot. An economy that has thrown itself at the mercy of finance, rather than building industry, is totally exposed. Everything the government now does and says is dictated, not by national needs or interests, but by the compulsion to pour more offerings on to the altar of confidence.

Growth is being damped before it can go on to save a declining economy. Britain is threatened because its industrial base is already too small. The means of national management, the methods of protection, the will to build national strength have all been deliberately abandoned. With imports of manufactures up fivefold since 1970 and exports only doubled, a surplus in manufactured trade equal to 4.9 per cent of GDP in 1970 has turned into a deficit of 3.3 per cent in 1988. That deterioration, over £37 billion at current prices, must get worse as the government's chosen methods of defence hit industry. We are drifting naked into the storm, committed to weapons that compound the problem, totally dependent on the fickle feelings of finance and foreigners. Britain is vulnerable, open to the world but unable to face it, dependent on it but unable to survive in it.

3

What Wasn't Said on the *Jimmy Young Show*: The Real Agenda

Anyone who judges Margaret Thatcher on Britain's decidedly mixed economic performance is being unfair. Her real programme was always political, and an economic miracle to reverse the decline that had brought her to power was not on the agenda. Haves prefer wealth ill-distributed. Levelling up by making the masses better off is against their instincts, and fast growth means stresses: strong unions, uppity workers, skill shortages, a need to cooperate, even an incomes policy. Growth is 'about' industry. The Conservatives are 'about' money and Thatcherism is 'about' discipline. So growth was an optional extra. If it came, well and good, particularly at election time, but the real programme was a moral one: a political counter-revolution. The promise of economic regeneration was an incidental; there were no policies to get it, beyond the Prime Minister's own faith and that particularly in herself. All that was needed was for her to impose her will and morality and all else would follow as the reward for virtue. The aim was not to rebuild but to take and keep power in order to impose that morality on a nation gone wrong.

Here was a political programme. Power was central to it, and the first requirement was to hang on to it long enough to carry through the revolution. The Conservative Party believes that it has a right to control the 'destinies of this great empire whether in government or in opposition', but it had managed to do so only intermittently since the war and then by espousing the welfare economy. Mrs Thatcher's was a new party with the New Blue additive: little noblesse, no oblige, men on the make with a lust for power heightened by new conviction politics. Being right, knowing the way, the truth, the life, she was dedicated to defeating the forces of evil.

A little help from the opposition, and a lot of luck from oil, gave politics a more settled mein, avoiding the reversals and humiliations of previous governments, and made Mrs Thatcher the first prime minister since Harold Macmillan not to live on a diet of her own words. Which was just as well. She had spoken all of them with such conviction that the spectacle of running against her own videotapes would have been comic. Yet her real skill was in holding her government together and driving it forward, preventing disunity, collapse and the suicide syndrome.

Her absolute conviction in her own rightness, always the prerogative of those who do not understand reality, sanctioned the digging in. The economy was managed for electoral purposes, generating buoyancy, as elections approached, deflating after. 'Real' disposable incomes in 1988 were 25 per cent up on 1978, underpinning everything with prosperity. While preaching stringency and discipline, the true strategy was lower taxes and better feelings now, at the expense of problems later – a live-now-pay-later system based on squandering oil, pumped up as if there would be no tomorrow, and gobbling the seed corn. This was government on tick. The savings ratio fell from 15 per cent of disposable income to 5 per cent, increasing consumer spending by 10 per cent and making the GDP 6 per cent higher. From 1985 to 1988 real incomes grew 3 per cent a year, consumer spending 6 per cent and consumer debt 12.5 per cent. Personal credit, £20.5 billion in 1980, had reached £282.8 billion in 1987, touching American levels but without the power of that economy behind it. Mortgage borrowing had the biggest boost of all, and much of it was syphoned off to meet consumer demand. At the start of the decade, the average individual's borrowing liabilities were 45 per cent of pretax income; by the end of 1987, they were 81 per cent.

Industry, too, ate its own capital. Investment was negative from 1979 to 1986, and by the end of that period, gross fixed capital formation was only 17 per cent at current prices, against 28 per cent in Japan. Leading the Gadarene rush, general government domestic capital formation fell 40 per cent over the decade, with another 6 per cent fall projected into the 1990s. Housing was cut back massively, pushing up prices of the declining stock and making home owners feel better off, at the cost of mounting problems. Cutting taxes by selling off public assets resulted in a return now, even at the cost of a tax increase later. Keeping the exchange rate artificially high ensured that a given quantity of British production bought more overseas. All these finite processes meant postponed problems, but elections are won here and now. Electoral success and economic folly are not incompatible, particularly for a government that had to stay in power to see its counter-revolution through.

That programme was aimed at destroying socialism. The balance of forces was to be reversed to ensure that it could never again be builded here. Critics portrayed this as social revenge to install the Ten-Year Reichette. In fact, it was dedicated to destroying socialism's bases. The economy was to be internationalized to make socialism in one country impossible. Britain was to be a land fit for investors, multinationals, finance and the movers and merchants of money, and power was handed to them from the state. In a national, industrial economy, Labour (with a capital L and without) was strong, skills were essential, industry was paramount, workers were proud and the Conservatives but one contender for power, having to pander to the proletariat and buy votes with benefits. The swing of the political pendulum was dominant. Because Labour would get to run the country intermittently, Tory achievement was reversible, and a Conservative government had to concentrate on people-pleasing, not on what was morally right.

However, plug Britain into international capitalism and all would be transformed. Labour and the unions were weak on the larger stage, the prey of more powerful forces than they could beat or manage. Socialism had to justify itself to a more prejudiced audience, and behave in a different fashion. The Conservatives would become the natural administrators of the new, talking the language of a world more theirs than Labour's and, by working with finance, would make it the Tory party at the VDU. Tories would no longer be forced to conciliate and bribe the workforce, nor to prop up British manufacturing. The constellation of forces would be changed.

Liberating the market reduced government's power. Opening up and internationalizing eliminated national controls. Finance and money, and those who have it, become dominant, managing credit and influencing interest rates and expansion, money supply and activity, instead of government. However, government is responsible and answerable. Finance operates by its rules – a.k.a. market rules – which suit those who have, rather than spoiling those who have not, for those who go into a market weak and vulnerable usually come out the same way. An inevitable part of this shift in power was a transfer from the state to some people, but hardly all.

The tax strategy symbolized and effected this. Taxes on top people were cut at the same time as they paid themselves more, for pay rises for the top fifth were 50 per cent greater than those for the bottom fifth. The cuts were paid for by reducing the amounts spent on benefits for those lower down. By 1988, the bottom half of the population had lost £6.6 billion, an average of £8.50 per family per week, in lower benefits and higher taxes. The top 10 per cent gained £5.6 billion, or £40 per family per week, of which £4.8 billion went to the top 5 per cent. Britain was becoming a meaner, more divided country, though in the government's view, the bottom was being given something to emulate, a model to rise to. The state was abandoning its redistributive role, and easing out of responsibility for those left behind.

The same was true of economic management. Balancing budgets meant that the state did not use its power to create credit. That was left to the banks to employ for their own purposes and profits. A government that made balanced budgets the centre of its strategy also had the perfect excuse for not increasing spending to deal with a depressed economy. Since the balancing was largely done by the confidence trick of selling assets, which count as negative public spending, the sales and the reduction of higher taxes both created a powerful inhibition on any later, Labour government. Once privatization was over, its revenues squandered, the government would be forced to increase taxes to compensate. Further increases to finance better services and restore redistribution would compound the problem. All this would remove the one competitive advantage that the Tories had provided – lower taxes – and would make Britain less attractive to foreign capitalism. Irresponsibility in the 1980s provided a brake on socialism in the 1990s.

Deficit financing was passed from the state to individuals, who borrowed on the appreciating asset of houses to provide their own deficits. Therefore, taking the nation out of debt meant plunging everyone else into it. It also concentrated economic management on high interest rates, driving the car without steering wheel or gears but only the brake. Industry suffered doubly as the exchange rate went up with higher interest rates. This made confidence, especially that of the financial community, crucial. It was yet another useful way of weakening Labour.

Everything that had preoccupied previous governments and at which they had failed – employment, output, growth, the balance of payments – could now be left to the market while the government watched the dials, particularly those measuring the money supply and the borrowing requirement, all of which meant managing for money, not production. The government was no longer responsible for building up national strength. It would claim credit for any improvement, but responsibility was handed to the market.

To help it, Britain was made a tax haven with low tax rates on capital, on business and on high earners to lure and keep them. That meant shifting the tax burden on to the less footloose factors known as the mass of the people. Thus company tax rates were reduced to 35 per cent on undistributed profits compared with 56 per cent in West Germany and 42 per cent in France, giving Britain the lowest taxes in the European Community and the winner in its competitive auction. Our top tax rate of 40 per cent is lower than anywhere else except Switzerland, but our starting point of 25 per cent is exceeded in only four countries, and the regressive indirect tax burden is one of the highest.

Britain was opened up to investors, to money flows, to multinational forces, to provide the regeneration, the investment, the new plants and processes, even the competition that the natives could not. So in yet another sphere, power passed from the British government and British interests to big money, financial flows, major multinationals, substantial investors and a financial sector that had been growing to dominance through the post-war period. Britain was becoming the kingdom of finance capitalism. That day in May 1979 marked its coronation, as well as Margaret Thatcher's. It would come, do well, work its magic; the benefits would trickle down to the people, in much the same way as a well-fed horse provides sustenance for the birds.

Tory rhetoric described this as 'setting the people free' or 'giving them more control'. In a credit society, they had to use the leverage of credit through the financial institutions. They were more exposed to the power of the latter because state credit, benefits and public spending, which would have created a better environment for them to stand on their own feet, were both reined back to give precedence to the private. The 'servile society' of Tory myth was replaced by an anxious one as debt pressed down and people became dependent on big impersonal institutions, their lives conditioned by the 'moralities' of finance. With fitting symmetry, Nigel Lawson's tax cuts were paid over, usually by direct debit and in even greater tribute, in higher interest rates to the merchants of greed.

The political bonus was that any future Labour government would be neutered. Labour would not be able to use the weapons of the 1960s and '70s: taxing capital, controlling finance, intervening, building the corporate state. The rules of the international game would stop any conspiracy with, or privilege to, British capital, so industry could no longer be bailed out. With taxes and wages below those of international competitors, future governments would have to keep them where they were to retain the foreign capital on which Britain had become dependent as it exported its own. With Britain plugged into international capitalism, anyone attempting to unplug it was guaranteed an electric shock.

Tories saw capitalism as the highest form of wisdom, its only problems being the workers, unions and governments. Weakened British capitalism would have to be whipped into shape by international competition, a natural assumption for a party that looked to the public school ethic of cold showers and regular punishment. With capital's rate of return brought up to international levels, industry could stand on its feet without the state. The first step was the abolition of exchange controls, making capital footloose. Those British firms not up to the mark would be starved of capital and go under. To survive, investment in Britain would have to earn the same rate of return on capital and make the same profits as competitors'. The 1979–81 deflation then provided the opportunity by closing firms that had been kept open in the hope of better times, inefficient, marginally profitable or even unprofitable firms that had coasted along, and a swathe of viable enterprises that would have been profitable and competitive if there had been a more realistic exchange rate, but would never be at the insane levels of 1979–81. This Great Liquidation closed a quarter of British productive capacity, £25 billion of it, made the rest more profitable as the prize for coming through, and set the capital free to go elsewhere – usually overseas.

A better rate of profit meant less dependence so government could slash all the benefits, grants and other help to industry introduced to compensate for failure. So everything went: regional grants, investment allowances, all forms of state support. The Department of Trade and Industry rushed to shed both its industrial role and instruments, and became as 'hands on' as a Saudi with two convictions for theft. Profitable industry could stand on its own feet, though the joy with which this should have been greeted by industrialists who had clamoured for that privilege was diminished by the heavier burdens of interest rates that they now had to bear. They then rushed to increase that burden by their scramble for leveraging, debt and takeovers.

Depression forced down the costs of the other factors of production, particularly labour. Tory analysis attributed Britain's failure to reduce high labour costs to restrictive labour practices, inefficient working, overmanning and the power of the trade unions. It was not true, but bringing down labour costs, or in Thatcher-speak 'letting people price themselves into jobs', was central to the strategy. Britain was to be turned into a low-wage economy. On the Council of Europe's 'Decency Threshold', defined as 68 per cent of full-time average earnings, Britain had 8 million, or 38 per cent of the workforce, below this level in 1979, 9.9 million or 47 per cent in 1988. Today the poorest fifth of manual workers earn less, relative to the average, than in 1886 when figures were first collected.

Deflation was the main weapon, supplemented by legal restrictions on unions much more subtle than Heath's 1971 backward-firing blunderbuss. The Tories of the 1980s were more cunning because they focused on picketing and abuses of union power, and introduced 'democracy' and ballots to which only those constipated by the rulebook could object. The restrictions were also more one-sided, taking away rights where Heath had conferred them, crippling union finances rather than creating martyrs, and throwing the unions on the mercy of Britain's reactionary judges rather than creating special labour courts where understanding might dilute prejudice. The Heath reforms had come in as rapid growth had begun, giving the unions the muscle to destroy both the reforms and the incomes policy that followed. The real reason why the Thatcher government was able to break the unions, while Heath's had been broken by them, was that the unions' muscle had been replaced by unemployment, making people frightened for their jobs, less likely to press for wage increases and more ready to make sacrifices to stay in work. Unions even had difficulty in demonstrating their worth, still less their power. The depression broke them, legal reforms then tied and trussed them and, finally, their Praetorian Guard, the miners, were broken as Arthur Scargill obligingly rushed into a carefully laid trap. Unions ended the 1980s with a 3 million fall in membership, a workforce questioning their value because they could not deliver, industrial power largely gone, the movement divided by growing competition for members.

A more compliant workforce was available to incoming investors. Employers could eliminate restrictive practices; management had the power to manage even if it was not very sure what to do. All was gained at a huge cost in bankruptcies, under-used resources, lost growth and productivity and the expense of unemployment, calculated in 1981 at £6000 per person in benefits paid and taxes lost. Yet in Britain's 'us and them' society, hurting the other side in the industrial war loomed larger than solving the problem because, to 'us', the other side *was* the problem. The 1980s became the decade in which British industry beat its own workforce but lost to the Germans.

This was not the high-wage, high-skill economy of a successful industry but a cheap-labour, low-cost failure, a tax haven for international capital. A nation with a pliant workforce in a weak bargaining position, reduced rights of job protection, and a restricted role for wage councils, which the government then proposed to abolish entirely. A general transition to casual, part-time non-unionized jobs. The government proclaimed a commitment to skills and new technology, but the Chancellor's 'low-skill – no-skill' preferences were clearer in a 'training' regime that was directed at unemployment register reduction, not skill inculcation, at the provision of cheap labour and increasingly reduced wage rates rather than re-skilling. Rather than putting pegs in the appropriate holes, it was reducing aspirations so the unemployed would accept lower-level, lower-paid jobs. The opportunity to upgrade was lost. The expansion of 1986–9 produced skill shortages at a depressingly early stage because Britain had failed to train enough people during the idle years.

Britain had now taken on a new role as Europe's Trojan Horse, where capital, finance, even manufacturing, could set up and have full access to Europe's markets. Mrs Thatcher was not a natural European. The European Community was fussy, interfering, semi-socialistic, and it had no control over its spending. Yet it gave British capital access to a huge market, and if it were run by the stern capitalist ethic of Rome rather than that of bureaucratic Brussels, an offshore-tax-haven-black-economy could benefit from membership. So the only aspects of the EC for which she showed any enthusiasm were deregulation and access – those calculated to make Britain a better base camp for an assault on Europe and attractive to foreigners. Britain offered everything: cheap labour, efficient capital markets and EC access for the Nissans, the Sonys, the Americans. The government and even the monarchy were prepared for any kow-tow that would bring them in.

In an open market, peripheries must offer special induce-
ments. A competitive currency and comparative advantage are
the best. The Conservative alternatives were lower taxation,
deregulation and cheap labour, and each in turn acted as a
guarantee that socialists would not be able to reverse any of
them. The competitive edge would be lost; capitalism and
capitalists would go elsewhere. Labour's hands were to be
tied.

The only ones not made privy to the plan were the British
people. They were puzzled by the razzamataz about '1992'
and the single market. Unions dreaded its effects on jobs.
Industry feared the increased competition. A few realists
wondered whether posters of Sir John Harvey-Jones about to
burp that 'History is in the faking' were an adequate prepara-
tion for something that other nations were carefully planning,
but the government was not prepared to do more. Certainly
not the detailed analysis about what to negotiate for, what
could be sacrificed and what the bottom line was. Neither
were they prepared to allocate the funds for the infrastructure
work necessary for success or to help regions certain to be
hard hit. Britain's approach showed all the sublime confidence
of 1972 in a situation where it was predictable that peripheries
would lose and the centre would gain unless government
countered the trends. None of this was important to Conservatives who had lost power in the peripheries and saw the
single market as the culmination of their internationalization
strategy: opening Britain to competition to keep British industry on its toes; allowing the European economy to be
dominated by large companies and British finance; offering
Britain up as an attractive, low-cost, low-tax base for an
invasion of Europe based on a new Mulberry, made in Japan.

'Setting free' involved transfers of power. Part of it was the
shift from government to big investors, the shock troops of
capitalism. They needed new opportunities. A central criterion
of investment is diversification to spread risk: 'Thirty stocks in
ten countries' was once the axiom, and the bigger the investor,
the greater the diversification. Investors, institutions and multi-
nationals had to be given their opportunities in Britain.

Privatization was the major instrument here. Unprofitable private capital was liquidated and replaced on the market by state assets. Investment policy in those nationalized industries had shown the way to private capitalism in the past. Their effectiveness was demonstrated as they slimmed down. The role of the state had been well justified on both counts, and had saved ailing firms such as Rover and Rolls Royce from bankruptcy and developed new technology such as Inmos. State industries were among the more efficient sectors of the economy, and even the less saleable ones such as British Steel, Rover and BR achieved minor miracles, though often by sale of assets, shedding labour and moving upmarket away from cooking steel, cooking cars and cooking travel to greater value added. Efficiency, manning levels, productivity and investment had all been improved to the point where they compared with the best foreign competition. Public ownership made this possible.

As a reward, they were sold in a programme of privatization that began small and became the biggest car-boot sale in history. The least attractive ones – the shipyards and Rover – went next to last, being allowed to fall off the back of the public sector on the Victor Kyam principle: 'You like the ships (or cars)? Have the shipyard (or the factory).' That gave British Aerospace massive balance-sheet gains. Private portfolios were diversified at no risk, new shareholders were lured in by a guaranteed pools win, foreign capital was tempted in – all by robbing the tax payer. The share price was pitched low to make sales successful and renationalization more difficult. Post-sale share prices all (except for BP) went up substantially – a loss to the tax payer. The costs of the programme were huge, most of it paid to the government's City and advertising cronies.

By January 1989, the government had made £25 billion gross; its total sales costs were £729 million and its advertising costs £66 million, all far greater than the costs of the equivalent quantity of gilts. The average increase in the share price after sale was 125 per cent or, in the case of Telecom, an increase from the £3.9 billion sale price to £8 billion, a capital gain of £4 billion on an asset that had once belonged to everyone.

This was the economics of irresponsibility. The real price

would be paid later when tax revenues would have to be increased to make good the loss of revenue. Low prices to keep down the cost of living, as under the Heath government, would be impossible. An increase in costs pressing on the economy was as inevitable as the way in which privatized monopolies exploited monopoly power. Compared to the American experience of trust busting, the British are amateurs at monopoly regulation: OFGAS and OFTEL are flexible checks, not real controls. Power and water faced the loss of the efficiency attained through public control: the efficient switching system; the national grid to bring in power stations at the point of maximum efficiency; the efficient scale of water provision bringing down the costs to industry. The charges of both were lower than those of most competitors, but are now certain to rise. Both were increased before, to fatten up the industries. In the case of British Steel, its efforts to generate profit and move downstream into stockholding precluded the kind of strategy that the Japanese used to provide cheap steel to make manufacturing competitive. They now all had to look after themselves; the government would not do it for them. Manufacturing would have to run its race tied to the ball and chain of higher external costs.

Prospective losses for political gains. Selling shares, particularly overseas, would make it more difficult for Labour to return assets to the public sector. Foreign investors might eventually pull out because their portfolio return on, say Korean steel was better than the return on British, but this threat, too, shackled Labour. The British rate of return had to be maintained.

Because the rate was made high in the 1980s, foreign capital poured in both for privatization and to buy up other assets. Britain was for sale, and competitors had open licence to buy. They got companies on the cheap as going concerns. Neither purchasers nor their subsidiaries faced any requirement to export, bring in research, design or development or do anything other than supply a British market that was profitable and open to rape. Meanwhile, instead of investing and producing, British capitalism used its overflowing cash for an orgy of takeovers and mergers. There were no gains in efficiency; all the academic studies showed an overall loss. There was a massive breaking of faith with those who had a stake in these companies, whether in the form of loyalty or job or as suppliers. Only quick profits for both aggressors and shareholders.

British capital poured out at a rate averaging 3 per cent of GDP a year, from funds, institutions, firms and private holders – over £10 billion most years making at least £120 billion to be sent for investment overseas, sometimes in assets, more often in portfolios, but all in the productive capacity of competitors. Britain was the second highest overseas investor after Japan, the biggest in the US alone. It was becoming a *rentier* economy, as interested in the success of others as of its own, a return to the late 19th century, with income flows keeping the pound higher than it would otherwise have been. This was providing for the future, the government said, but it was really providing for the futures of those who owned the capital, and even that was not guaranteed: in October 1987, the value of Britain's overseas investments fell by a third.

For British capitalism to be rebuilt, cheap money and a competitive pound are essential. Yet internationalization guarantees the reverse. To keep the money coming in, high interest rates are essential. With Britain plugged into the world's money system and not in control of its own, the government put the pound up, bringing even more money in. Successful economies are prepared to lend us more to ensure that we continue buying their goods. So the money supply in Britain rises as the price of money goes up, and to sustain confidence, that then has to go even higher. Treasury Bill rates in Britain have been consistently double those in West Germany.

Dear money, a high pound, high interest rates – all suited finance and made investment overseas cheap. They weakened domestic industry and transferred power to the Bank of England, for in an open economy, monetary policy governs the external balance, fiscal policy the internal. Since the government had abandoned fiscal policy and interest rates were determined by the movement of international capital, monetary policy was, in effect, determined by the central bank, managing its portfolio through its open market operations. It could veto the government's economic policies, just as it had done until 1931. The inevitable consequences were never spelled out. The weapons of insulation and economic nation-building that every other industrializing country had used were gone. The government could not even use the weapons that had given Britain its own inadequate growth since the war. The staples of post-war strength were abolished to throw Britain open to the world.

In 1944, John Maynard Keynes told the House of Lords of the government's plans for post-war economic management:

The experience of the years before the war has led most of us, though some of us late in the day, to certain firm conclusions. Three, in particular, are highly relevant to this discussion. We are deter-mined that, in future, the external value of sterling shall conform to its internal value as set by our own domestic policies, and not the other way round. Secondly, we intend to retain control of our domestic rate of interest, so that we can keep it as low as suits our own purposes, without interference from the ebb and flow of inter-national capital movements or flights of hot money. Thirdly, whilst we intend to prevent inflation at home, we will not accept deflation at the dictate of influences from outside. In other words, we abjure the instruments of bank rate and credit contraction operating through the increase of unemployment as a means of forcing our domestic economy into line with external factors.

None of that remained. Britain was exposed and particularly vulnerable without a strong industry. The end result was to make Britain a branch economy, not the home of a powerful national exporting machine. Unable to be richer than the world, it would tag along behind.

If the new dependence did not work, the government would not be to blame. The Prime Minister had done all that morality required, and travelled the world selling British arms and contracts promoting Britain's image through her own. The blame for failure would rest with those who were not worthy of her: lazy workers; unenterprising bosses; greedy finance; incompetent exporters; Luddite unions; soft management. While privatizing everything else, Margaret Thatcher had na-tionalized alibis, all reserved for the government. All this constituted a counter-revolution far more important than the economic strategies and much more successful. Political balances had been swung to the Conservatives and nailed down. The bases of opposition had been undermined, and the weapons it would look to in the unlikely event of power had been weakened or rendered obsolete. Socialism, Labourism, expansionism in one country had all been made more difficult if not impossible. Instead of shackling, the state had been shackled. The Conservatives had been dug into power.

The downside was that the state was rolled back by increasing its power. It became more dominant because countervailing powers – trade unions, local government, universities, independent broadcasting – were weakened. Britain's economy had been left exposed in a harder, colder, more competitive world. The corporate techniques of defence and management that others still used had been outlawed along with socialism.

The whole philosophy of removing government from industry had really been imported from the United States. This may, doubtfully, have been relevant in a powerful continental economy with a mighty industrial machine. It was far less so in a vulnerable economy whose industry was in decline because it had lost out to corporate competition from national champions working with their governments in collusion against the world. Indeed, the market was likely to relegate the whole country because markets compound decline and drain a periphery. They strengthen the strong, just as 'free trade' had done for Britain. They are less good for sick economies.

Yet Britain had been chained to the most fickle and destructive of these markets: international financial flows. With the abandonment of exchange control, these became the dominant influence on interest rates and hence the all-important exchange rate. The economy was awash with money, but being too dear for productive investment, it was channelled into asset inflation. The pound was pushed up, so the current account went into deficit, a minor image of capital account in surplus. The exchange rate exacerbated the trade imbalance instead of correcting it by coming down, turning a productive economy that paid its way in the world into a financial bingo game. Exposed to more powerful competitors, groaning under finance's burdens, bereft of government's protection and cooperation, manufacturing could not close the gap. Margaret Thatcher was not running a sanitorium but an Outward Bound economy. She had no idea of what to do if that did not work. Unfortunately, it did not.

Power is the test of success or failure for politicians. On that basis, Margaret Thatcher has been the most successful prime minister of the century. She has held it without let or hindrance, used it vigorously to impose her prejudices and made it difficult for opposition to reverse what had been done. Where others try to achieve balance, she has unbalanced; she has broken labour, done down industry, weaned land to make it dependent on a drying Brussels teat, and enthroned finance. No longer *primus inter pares*, the government literally gave it power. There was to be no balance that a new government could renegotiate but an enforced dominance of one over all.

Such are the crude political tests. Perhaps it is unworthy to ask a near-divine figure what she can do for her country, but the Thatcher interest is not necessarily the national interest, and Britain must apply the tests of economic success and strength. Has she 'enlarged the nation and increased our joy'? Her electorate has been given the choice between two pictures: a Dorian Gray, painted and regularly retouched by the Walworth Road Studios; and a Gainsborough, painted by numbers at the Ingham Art School. The first is a picture of national decline and failure, the other of success, rising living standards, re-dedication and transition to a superior service economy, leaving metal bashing to yellow races while Britain becomes a post-industrial, high-tech information society. A confusing contrast. A doubting electorate is incapable of making the choice because they decide only by effects on their lives.

Growth has been steady for five years, the improvement in living standards even greater. Yet in the light of the opportunities that oil could have brought, both have been small, particularly when compared to the needs of a nation in long-term decline, which requires the massive boost that competitors have enjoyed. Nations live or die by the strength of their industrial economies. Britain's has been weakened. The task was to make Britain strong, by rebuilding industry, but the Tory years have proved disastrous. Monetarism weakened industry; internationalizing exposed it. Industry is national and looks to demand on the domestic market. Overvaluation transferred much of that to imports. Industry needed the same backing and support that competitors were getting from their governments. Britain's government cut support, abolished subsidy and tax encouragement, cut industry adrift and imposed the double burden of high interest rates and overvaluation, seeing foreign competition as a discipline and a way of defeating inflation.

The dominance of finance meant dear money, short-term perspectives and a continuous need for industry to protect its own back. Any firm that invested in long-term development saw its share price fall and the threat of take-over grow, unlike the US, where high-tech adventures are encouraged, or other nations where the banks support them. Since British industry raised more of its capital in shares and never had as protection a close relationship with the banks, unlike West German, Japanese or French industry, or with government – local, regional or even national – it was vulnerable to take-over, while the funds and institutions that held 70 per cent of equities between them are always open to a quick profit. Rather than sticking with companies, they *have* to sell to perform on the short-term indices by which their success is measured. Instead of building for the future, industry was eating itself, not only in the take-over war but also because gross domestic fixed capital formation fell by 17 per cent in real terms from 1979 to 1987. There was a net disinvestment in industry for the first time, and all too much of the investment that did occur went into defence, prestige projects, company cars, electronic dealing rooms, estate agencies and supermarkets – not into the machinery and production that would allow us to win and hold manufacturing markets. Here, with a few exceptions such as chemicals and pharmaceuticals, our record was the worst in the advanced world. Investment by manufacturing is still not back to the level of 1979.

Manufacturing's contribution to the GNP and employment declined from over a third in the 1960s to under a quarter. It shed 3 million jobs in the process, 2 million of them under Margaret Thatcher, a decline far greater than that in any other country, and a symptom of a unique industrial failure. Some countries, including Japan, were still increasing manufacturing employment. Elsewhere, it declined only proportionately because industry was so successful that it could produce more with fewer. Nor was Britain closing down old industries to bring on the new: our old industries were being beaten by the old industries of more efficient competitors, primarily in the EC, from whence have come three-quarters of the increased imports of manufactures since 1980. Britain was closing industry down, and losing capacity because industry was failing. That was a unique national disaster. Manufacturing output at factor cost had risen 67 per cent from 1957 to 1973. It fell by 4 per cent from 1973 to 1987 (14 per cent if industries more sheltered from competition, such as defence, are excluded), and got back to 1979 levels only by its belated spurt in 1988. The average annual rate of growth of manufacturing – 3 per cent from 1957 to 1967, 3.5 per cent from 1967 to 1973 – was almost nil from 1979 to 1987.

By 1987, imports of manufactures comprised 54 per cent of British industry's own sales to its home market, comparing disastrously with 35 per cent in 1979, or with 25 per cent in West Germany and France today. Such increases work on a ratchet basis: once gained, they are difficult to roll back. Entrepreneurs are increasingly reluctant to risk capital to defeat them. Industry has all too little opportunity to reach up to the scale essential for survival. It competes from sinking sands. Our exports of manufactures rose only 5.5 per cent while world trade rose 8.5 per cent, so Britain's share of world trade in manufactures was down to 7 per cent, a third of West Germany's. The former workshop of the world had become a guzzling importer of manufactures, and a warehouse for their distribution.

Because manufacturing cannot pay the nation's way, everything now has to be squeezed down. Industry had to invest to survive but high interest rates crippled that. As a result, it did not invest, develop R&D or train adequately to renew itself. So the nation was relegated, its future undermined. Many economists were in favour of increasing integration, doubtful about the viability of national economies. Yet successful integration implies a contribution that others want. What was happening in Britain was a collapse. We were defeated by more powerful competitors, particularly West Germany. The world was a battle ground of national competitors. We had lost out.

4

From the British Disease to Rigor Mortis?

Britain is in decline because the industrial engine is neither strong enough nor big enough to haul the nation forward. Long years of comparative decline have made industry weak and vulnerable and have narrowed the industrial base. Thatcherite shock treatment compounded the damage. Now the engine can no longer do its job, unlike its counterparts in more advanced competitor nations. No alternative has been developed. Relegation results. Society becomes meaner and the public sector smaller and shabbier, not only because both suffer from Margaret Thatcher's grudge against post-war Britain but also because these are the inevitable consequences of decline.

Three broad alternative solutions were attempted in two decades. The first: Go for growth to burst through the constraints. The second: Subsidize, cosset and support industry to keep it going. The third: Make some of it profitable, sink the rest and make the poor bear the sacrifices. Heath opted for the first, Labour for the second, Mrs Thatcher for the third. The first bubble burst even more quickly than Nigel Lawson's oil-fired effort. The second ended in Luddite revolt. The third leads to a divided and colonized economy. None solves Britain's problems.

That requires us to tackle the central problem: rebuilding and broadening industry by managing the economy to sustain competitiveness and then providing all the backing and co-operation it needs to expand and grow, increase output and widen its range back into the huge areas where it has been defeated, or has never developed. Nigel Lawson's unbalanced boomlet has shown that industry can grow, however hindered.

The balance-of-payments problem was the government's responsibility, not industry's; the finger points directly at the high exchange-rate policy. High growth should have been sustained. Britain's need is to rebuild industry before the tightening balance-of-payments constraint strangles everything here, and intensifying competition closes doors abroad. The compounding processes of failure lead but to the grave. Only with the industrial engine rebuilt and repaired can Britain go on to build the better society. Without that, everything else is futile. So is Britain.

Thatcherism means despair. It will not work and blocks everything that can. Yet other nations have built and rebuilt powerful economies. So did Britain after the Great Depression. That, unlike Britain's present problem, was international, but like today's, it was caused by financial instabilities, not industrial failure. The creditor countries beggering the world 70 years ago were France, with an undervalued currency, and the US, holding most the world's debts. Today, they are Japan and West Germany with their surpluses and their refusals to allow their exchange rates to appreciate to the necessary degree. The effect on Britain has been the same.

Many socialist myths are made in the United States. Contrary to a prevalent one, in economic terms capitalist Britain had a good depression, followed by a good war. Other nations elected radical reforming governments that used the power of the state to protect the people: Roosevelt's New Deal, New Zealand Labour's 1935 election victory leading to insulation of the economy and the welfare state; the rise of the Swedish SAP with a similar mission; the belated arrival of the Australian Labour Party. All made change immediate and substantial. As a result, a legend was born that socialism cured depression, and like so much else, we imported it.

In Britain, Labour was in office but not in power as the Great Depression hit. That circumstance gave birth to a long Labour tradition of holding things together by sticking to orthodoxy and respectability in a way that the Conservatives have never bothered with. The strain tore the party apart. The Conservatives came in, suitably disguised as the National government, to take a series of daringly radical measures. They went off the Gold Standard, which Labour had defended with its life. 'They never told us we could do that,' said former Labour ministers, but it brought an effective devaluation of over 30 per cent. To ensure that the pound remained low rather than bouncing back, the government created an Exchange Equalisation Account, which increased by 1935 to almost 13 per cent of the GNP, so great was the need to keep the pound down to sustain the new-found competitiveness of British industry. Imperial Preference was imposed with a tariff of 10 per cent on imported manufactures. Cheap money reduced bill rates below 0.5 per cent. Accompanied by a compulsory reduction of rates on government debt and an enormous increase in the money supply, it meant that government had taken control of finance. This was classic Keynes. He approved.

Roosevelt's lurching interventionism was more muscular and history-book-grabbing, but unlike Britain's efforts, it did not go to the heart of the matter, which was the control of finance. The problem was not industry but the unstable financial atmosphere in which it was asked to work. Britain's unsung New Deal grasped that central issue. Others tinkered with the real economy and were less successful. On the key test, unemployment fell more rapidly here than anywhere else, declining by over half between 1931 and 1937: 2.62 million jobs were created, 1.4 million of them in manufacturing. By 1936, production was 38 per cent up on the 1929 peak. The British Car industry trebled production and surpassed the French. Exports rose rapidly. Imports were held. The economy roared into a new life, doing more to solve the social problems of depression than all the welfare measures inaugurated elsewhere.

Expansion shaped a new nation with its ring roads, factory estates, new suburbs and New Towns, art deco factories, new electrical, chemical and artificial fibre industries. This was the most successful period of economic resurgence in British history. The sustained rate of growth, 5–6 per cent for several years, has not been exceeded since, and not by other countries at the time. Nor has the record number of jobs created – the equivalent of 800,000 a year for five years on today's figures.

The car industry, engineering, ship building, all the basic sinews revived, accompanied by the new industries: electronics, radio, television, radar, aviation. A powerful industrial economy, able to take on the burdens of rearmament and war, was built. Without that, Britain's fate during the coming conflict might have been very different.

We need the same regeneration today, but with a more massive boost for the real level of unemployment is higher and more of it long term, and there is a bigger backlog of industrial damage and a more pressing need for expansion into new areas. Yet some of the previously successful methods are now ruled out: tariffs by GATT, others by the European Community, protectionism by the climate of economic opinion. Although the world is now more interdependent, Britain's problem is unique – a hulk in a powerful fleet. Yet the reality is the same as it was in the 1930s: loss of jobs from industry caused by failure of demand, a failure now restricted to British production, but still caused by overvaluation. That of the '20s was imposed by Churchill's misguided decision to go back to gold at the pre-war parity. Today's is institutional; both hindered exports boosted imports.

Where, before, the approach was interventionist, today regeneration should emphasize market management: make the pound competitive and expansion will follow. Markets will develop what is profitable, and the expansion will spread to the rest of the economy. This is working with the dynamics of the system, but to the same problem – inadequate demand – there is only the same solution: curing the deficiency by a massive boost, so that the natural regenerative forces of a capitalist economy can bring back the jobs. What the market has taken away by lack of competitiveness, only the market can bring back by restoring it.

Nor is there any alternative but to rebuild industry, old fashioned, messy and inconvenient though many find it. It is what we have lived by, and must again. Nothing else offers. Finance can supplement the national income, but not provide jobs. Services are parasitic on industry. Public-sector jobs are financed by taxes. Industry alone can set the people back to work, doing what they did before or something like it, widening and deepening its spread to compensate for the fact that manufacturing will never again be as labour intensive as it once was. No use hoping for a sudden crop of new technological industries, springing fully armed from the head of Lord Young. The new grows out of the old. If it came Phoenix-like from ashes, that would be the only justification for this government's policy of ash creation, but it does not, needing the sustaining network of training, skills, investment and suppliers to be able to breathe again. Unless industry flourishes, nothing new comes, for only weeds grow in graveyards. We cannot consume without producing, and having become addicted to goods we once made here, we can only buy them if we also make them again.

The methods of rebuilding are, as in the 1930s, really dictated by the problem. First, insulate the economy. Then boost demand, having ensured that it fuels British production and jobs rather than washing overseas to buy imports. Only insulation and the promise to sustain it provide the incentive to invest in Britain and export from it. Otherwise, imports have too firm a grip on the market to be rolled back. Who will risk capital in the fruitless struggle to repel them? No industrial economy has ever been built, or rebuilt, when exposed to the full blast of more powerful competition in an open market. Without some respite from the storm, British industry will not invest, grow or, possibly, even survive.

Insulation can now be provided only by the exchange rate – tariffs are ruled out by the EC and, in any event, would produce retaliation. Devaluation means the price mechanism to make imports dearer, exports cheaper and more profitable, giving some of the same incentive to Britain's internationally traded sector that others have used to trigger off their virtuous cycles of growth. Expansion of exports attracts investment to existing industry by offering it opportunity, thus increasing productivity, and opening up economies of scale as well as giving industry the ability to improve research, design, development and all the other non-price factors in competitiveness, which, in fact, depend on price because all have costs to be financed out of profits.

The rate against the Deutschmark is 50 per cent up in real

terms on 1976 when we promised the IMF that we would maintain the competitive position of British manufactures at home and abroad. That rise must be reversed, requiring a devaluation of one-third to correct the market distortion and return our competitive situation to where it was, to restore the ground lost. Only devaluation can break that ratchet of a high exchange rate sustained by high interest rates, which has crippled British industry. New investment and confidence need the guarantee of sustained competitiveness to make this country a powerful base to manufacture in and export from, and to replace imports on the home market. There is no need, however, to set devaluation targets in advance, or even talk about the issue. The pound will come down substantially with a change of government and can always be talked and helped down. All that is required is to be bold and undercut finance's inevitable attempt to make money by bidding it down further and then to keep it down by tying the exchange rate to the monthly terms of trade for manufactured goods to stay competitive.

With the environment for growth created and made permanent by a government locking itself to competitiveness and eating the key, rather than its own words, demand can be expanded massively. Private credit would have to be properly regulated, by requiring banking institutions to make deposits with the Bank of England which are geared to the finance they provide for jobs and investment as distinct from asset speculation; in this way, the government can direct credit. Labour should not give itself a Scrooge image, moralistically deploring consumer spending, but should channel private and expand public credit. The latter is more directly effective in producing jobs, while expansion of benefits for the poor goes directly into demand: unlike tax cuts, it is spent quickly and mainly on British goods. A public-sector deficit in place of the job-destroying surplus allows an increase in public spending, pumping out money through works and benefits.

This government has a horror of borrowing which is totally unjustified. The question of whether to run a deficit or a surplus is one that should be decided by the state of the economy. If resources are underemployed, a deficit is the only way to boost the economy, as President Reagan has shown, and the only arguments against it are moral, not economic. It can be financed by borrowing, by unfunded debt as in the 1930s, by requiring the banks to make deposits with the Bank of England and to buy government debt, and, with discretion, by using government credit. Why should the banks alone monopolize money creation?

Struggling to control the money supply is as unrealistic as it is unnecessary. It was cut massively under Labour and has been held well below required growth levels by the Tories. So boost it. Money created is spent to stimulate demand, sent abroad to bring down the exchange rate, or saved to bring down interest rates. All are beneficial. The only climate that will produce expansion and investment in British industry will be a boost to demand so massive that the prospects cannot be ignored. Industry then will have no alternative but to invest, to train, to break the bottlenecks that would otherwise strangle expansion. Without that effort, industry will fall further back and become locked in at even lower levels. To break out, the boost must be massive and sustained, so that industry will grasp the opportunity.

Finance, with its short-term, selfish interests, has been dominant for far too long. For industry to be rebuilt, finance must be 'less proud', as Winston Churchill put in in 1925, and industry 'more content'. That means managing money rather than running the economy for finance. It also means giving finance direct state competition from a national investment bank and a national enterprise board, to provide long-term investment and the money for reorganizing, rebuilding and expanding. Money must be the servant, not the master. The state has an obligation to manage it for public purposes, not leave everything to the banks to manipulate for theirs.

The safeguard that prevents expansion from ending in inflation and overheating is the social cooperation that the Conservatives are loath to attempt. They do not trust the unions. They prefer discipline to laxity. 'When in doubt, deflate' is their motto. It takes social management to ease growth's pressures. Only a party with social skills, prepared to work with the people and the unions, can face real growth. A mass training scheme, government financed, should boost skills, initially through pressure-cooker courses, later through the long-term re-skilling and upgrading that is vital.

Regional policy and incentives, preferably through regional employment premiums and job subsidies, should spread the growth round the country to avoid all of it concentrating in the South-east. An anti-inflationary strategy based on a corporate national economic assessment, bringing together the unions, government and employers can sustain confidence and generate cooperation – not an incomes policy alone, but an agreement that, if inflation is in danger of spiralling out of control, the government will act through subsidies, the unions through incomes policy, the employers through restraint. Inflation results from any attempt to expand, just as it does in decline. The problem is to stop it taking off.

This programme is straightforward. It uses techniques developed by other nations in economic nation-building. It goes with the economic grain, working by market forces and the price mechanism, but by managing the market, not abdicating to it. It makes British industry an offer it can't refuse and uses the dynamics that have produced previous bursts of growth, while taking steps, this time, to sustain them. It tackles the essence of the problem by rolling back the tide of imports, and combining that with export-led growth to improve our dwindling share of world trade.

Industry will respond, as it did in the 1930s, in the Heath Boom and in the Lawson Boomlet. It needs support – help to break the bottlenecks and ease the inflationary pressure – as well as the removal of the burdens of high interest and overvalued sterling, plus the guarantee that expansion will be sustained. A government riding out threats to sterling, allowing the exchange rate to go down rather than propping it up and determined to maintain competitive terms of trade can make expansion the paramount aim of policy. Nor would it be disruptive internationally. Devaluation is perfectly acceptable, though there would be pressure to get the pound back up to eliminate our new-found competitiveness as it threatens industrial rivals. World trade is not zero-sum but ever-expanding. Britain can increase its shrunken share as the Americans are now doing, and as the industrializing countries have all done. We are not now important enough for the world to feel threatened by a resurgent British industry. A minimal improvement, half of the ground lost over the last 15 years, would replace all the jobs that have disappeared.

President Reagan's deficit financing has created 10 million jobs. As the last Keynesian who had not gone grey, he realized the fundamental principle of economic management: Get the growth and the jobs, hang the consequences. Growth is the only way of defeating inflation; jobs the only formula for the good society. The consequences can all be coped with. All this can be done in Britain and should be, for there can be no solution, no socialism, no better society without this. Industry is the engine of the nation, and the only basis for survival and national strength. Only sustained growth can trigger the long-delayed British economic miracle and allow it to break through to continuous improvement.

A noble dream – which will not happen. When nations built their economies, they were responding to overwhelming national needs. Their populations were ready to accept discipline and stringencies. Britain is a satiate society, though without its sustaining base. A pluralistic society addicted to imports is impossible to mobilize. There is no consensus on what to do. Too many discount industry: it has 'had its day'. Politicians and pundits disagree on both the problem and the diagnosis. There is no lobby for growth, but a powerful one for inertia and imports.

Unless the industrial economy is rebuilt, Britain will decline further into irrelevance, unable to pay its way or support either a reasonable standard of living or a large population. Yet these remote threats are vague worries, not directly motivating pressures. The British see little need for the national effort required. There is no build-up of forces to generate or support it. The public senses that all is not well. It resents the collapse of jobs, factories, skills. It fears unemployment. But it also thinks that there is something inevitable about all this, and it has not, as yet, experienced any of the horrendous consequences of collapse. The nation has been fed comforting rubbish for so long that it has almost begun to believe it. It might respond to leadership but gets none because its leaders are on the wrong auto-pilot or are reading the polls to find what the public wants, not deciding what it needs. Even in the 1930s, the National government did not boldly trail what it intended. To attack finance and certainties long construed as moral laws might have been too frightening. It asked for, and got, a doctor's mandate, and then did what was necessary. How much more difficult, then, the job of opposition today, proposing policies to deal with the hard realities of the later 1990s to an electorate made nervous by the 1970s and affluent by the 1980s.

A coalition of vested interests holds power. Its sovereign is finance, which sees its interests as the nation's and operates worldwide. The courtiers are importers, distributors, the European bureaucracy, the propaganda machinery sustained by it and all the soft-faced men who have done well out of decline. Wealthier consumers want choice and prefer imports. If people will not buy British to save jobs, and if they spend redundancy money on imported videos and cars, they will not defend the remaining jobs with much vigour. The dominant coalition and the orthodoxies it preaches all point to a nation hooked on its own decline.

This makes action more difficult. What makes it impossible is that political deadlock is reinforced by structural problems. In the 1930s, Britain was one of four big, dominant economies. International coordination and institutions were weak and Britain was fairly free to act. Today, it is tied in by international agreements such as the GATT, by international consultations and the 'special relationship' with the United States. Even great powers, which today means only the US, find difficulty in doing what they want, though they still can. Those hanging on by their fingertips to the status of a power must conform more assiduously to retain it. We are the archetypal Boy Scouts, the supreme conformists, but unless we help ourselves, no one will help us. International arrangements compound national problems because they require nations in trouble to deflate their domestic economies. The old Bretton Woods exchange-rate arrangements required deflation of debtors but imposed no adjustments on creditors such as West Germany and Japan. Aid from the IMF, the World Bank or the central banks requires deflation, again compounding failure on the failing. There is no hope from outside. Only intensifying competition to compound problems, and the dynamics of open markets to drain peripheries.

As a member of the European Community, we are no longer our own masters. Self-help hurts the EC and breaks its rules. Despite these constraints, we could still do some necessary things: there is freedom of action for those with the sense and determination to use it, especially the original members for whom the rules were drawn up. Yet the EC heightens internal inertia, making decisions more difficult and less likely. A decision on what to do about our membership in the EC must be taken before we can decide on what to do about Britain – a hierarchy of decisions for a nation incapable of any, creating a psychological dependence and a decision deadlock, both of which palsy action. The EC shackles Britain to its decline. What started out as a solution to the problem has become the major part of it.

Our EC membership is based on confusion, dreams and lies, the characteristics of a country ignorant of economic realities. The ignorant are incapable of a single-minded pursuit of their own interests, and in that respect, the EC merely handcuffs Britain to the consequences of its own follies. Their basis is Britain's divided society. The divisions in divided nations blame each other and calculate advantage by reference to each other, and so it was that when Britain agreed to join the European Economic Community (as it was then called), membership heightened decline.

The Establishment, plus a Foreign Office that represented foreigners and a generation that had seen greatness – mostly viewed the EC as a new stage to strut on. Politicians who had failed to deliver economic success hoped to abdicate responsibility to it. Farmers wanted automatic support, not to be part of a scrum clamouring for subsidy from Parliament. Treasury saw it as getting farming's growing burden off the taxpayer's back and on to the consumer's. The Civil Service thought Europe would defer to Oxbridge chaps. Business wanted to castrate the workers and their unions. None saw the overall problem, certainly not industry which, if it thought at all, opted for the easy images of public school cold showers and competitive sports. James Meade's theory of customs unions – which demonstrated that not all can benefit, and that it was possible that none would, depending on the amount of trade created and the amount diverted – was hardly heeded. Few bothered to realize that competitiveness would be even more necessary to seize benefits in the larger market than it had been necessary – but never secured – in the world we were losing. Open markets imply access to ours. We were taking down a higher tariff against them than theirs against us. It is easier to penetrate a small market from a larger than vice versa, given the comparative costs of setting up distributorships and trading networks.

We had asked to be clobbered, but were still surprised when we were. Policy makers neither understood nor cared what would happen to output and employment in British industry because they neither understood nor cared about British industry. In practice, our rate of growth would have had to rise dramatically to compensate for the huge increase in the price of food that was bound to press on all our costs, and to finance a contribution to the EC which was certain to be disproportionately large because it would be geared to the needs of agriculture, not to our standard of living or to the strength of our economy. That rise in growth never came. The contribution bill did. Our exports to the other member countries had to increase much faster than our imports to compensate for the loss of tariff preferences in the Commonwealth and EFTA and for the severance of trading links with food-producing countries. They did not. Instead, EC exports to us rose rapidly.

Set an impossible task, we inevitably failed. In 1970, we had a surplus with the then EEC on trade in manufactures of about £4 billion at present values. The 1988 deficit is £14–15 billion, an £18 billion turn-around representing over 1 million jobs exported to Europe, to which can be added another half a million due to the loss of exports to non-member countries consequent on the change in our trading relationships. Trade with Europe has increased, but the EC share of our job-creating exports of manufactures has gone up from 31 per cent in 1970 to only 46 per cent in 1987 while the EC share of our job-destroying imports of manufactures has risen from 35 per cent to 56 per cent. Nearly four-fifths of the total increase in imports of manufactures of 450 per cent between 1970 and 1987 came from the EC, which increased its share of our market from 6 per cent to 20 per cent. Our share of the EC's imports of manufactures fell from 8.2 per cent to 7.8 per cent. Unless that balance is reversed and we win back our own market, by getting the level of manufactured imports down to the same proportion it is in France and West Germany (roughly half ours), there is no prospect of rebuilding Britain.

A second burden is the Common Agricultural Policy (CAP) and the budgetry contributions it gives rise to because EC financing is based on agriculture and food levies. The extra cost of the CAP, as against buying food on the cheapest market, is now over £13.50 a week for the average family of four. The only fair basis for contributions should be the national ability to pay, but British government has not tried to shift them on to this basis, and our complaints of 'unfair' have been met with temporary rebates. This creates dependency for, unless we comply on other issues, the pathetic rebate is threatened. Even with it, our 1989 budget contribution will be £2.0 billion net, a heavy price for a nation with a balance-of-payments deficit to pay.

Another burden is the costs of open markets. Conservatives like markets because they help the strong, a process only the state can correct. So it is with open trading markets. They drain life, jobs and development away from peripheries, particularly if these are already in decline. Prevailing trends are compounded: the strong get stronger, the weak weaker, and growth focuses on the centres of population and wealth, which means Europe's Golden Triangle, extending now to include northern Italy but not us. Britain is a periphery and certain to lose out still more as the 'single market' removes remaining barriers and the Channel Tunnel speeds the disaster.

A nation-state can buck such processes by using its powers and the 40 per cent (or more) of the GDP passing through its hands to offset market dynamics through regional aid, benefits, contracts, infrastructure work. The EC has no corresponding central structures. Less than 1 per cent of Europe's GDP passes through the Community's hands, and that for redistribution mainly to agri-business. Its regional aid is our own money returned to us with EC strings attached, and though the Regional Fund has been increased by 80 per cent in real terms, the claims of the poorer Mediterranean countries are stronger than ours: one-third of the assisted regions are in Spain and Portugal. Regions are rated as 'lagging' (the majority) or 'declining industrial' (like ours) now cut to 20 per cent of the structural funds. Nothing here to offset the damage.

We should come out but cannot. The EC has failed us, but the parties avoid the issue. The Democrats moan at specific EC follies, but ultimately believe in 'my market right or wrong' because they are European federalists. Conservatives are deeply ambivalent. Their leader tries for – and gets – the best of all possible worlds by beating the anti-market drum for the domestic audience yet she always goes along, grumbling, with developments she cannot stop because they've got her by the rebates. The vested interests – farmers, importers, finance (which hopes to see London as the EC's financial capital) and the hard-faced men who have done well out of the market – are all Tory and do not mind others suffering for their benefit. Labour decided on withdrawal by an overwhelming majority in 1981 and featured it in the 1983 manifesto, but its leadership never argued the case, assuming, as a kind of self-fulfilling prophecy, that withdrawal was unpopular, which it is if the case is never put. The discontents were never mobilized. It came to be seen as respectable among the Labour leadership to march backwards into the EC, emphasizing the social market and showing a communitaire enthusiasm that Labour voters certainly do not share, all the better to attack Mrs Thatcher.

In giving up the anti-market card, Labour has left a major section of opinion unrepresented. During the last six months in 1988, 47 per cent of the people opposed membership compared to 33 per cent in favour. The majority want out but may be too nervous to vote for it, having been told for so long that Britain is finished on its own. This is the final hypocrisy: a nation that does not like being in will not vote for the exit or for a party that proposes it. The only effective approach is political double-speak: Margaret Thatcher has mastered it.

The restraints imposed by EC membership increase all the

time. Measures necessary to rebuild industry are either precluded or questionable in an EC context. Several have already been struck down: the Regional Employment Premium; the £20 million scheme for restructuring the woollen industry; zero VAT on new construction; state aid for Rover; origin marking as information for the consumer. A national investment bank would infringe Community law if it provided preferential loans to exporting industry. The expansion of regional policy or employment premiums and subsidies to increase employment would be out. So would the 'Marks & Spencer' purchasing-and-contract policy that Labour proposed to encourage investment and R&D. Any state support for industries, whether nationalized or not, or any aid that discriminates in favour of our industry against that of any member of the EC, any attempt to check or control dumped or disruptive imports from third parties, or any MITI-type strategy to cooperate with industry and build market share – indeed, aid to restructure industry in any way could be struck down.

Expansion needs investment, and investors cannot afford uncertainty. Yet if measures can be contested by importers and policies overruled by British courts where any of them conflict with EC regulations, there is no secure base on which to build. All this will be made more difficult by the single market, precluding most non-tariff barriers and opening public contracts and financial and professional services – even defence, the best protected industry of all – to the same kind of competition that manufacturing has faced and has, in part, succumbed to.

It is not yet clear whether we will join the Exchange Rate Mechanism of the European Monetary System (EMS), but the odds are that we will have to before 1992. Nigel Lawson and the Treasury, the media and the CBI want to join. Mrs Thatcher, right but for the wrong reasons, does not. Yet she may be prevailed on to go in as a counter in negotiation or as a price for the deregulation she wants. The argument is that full membership of the EMS will help exports by stopping exchange-rate fluctuations. Yet no study shows that these have damaged trade, and whatever helps exports also helps imports. Our real problem is overvaluation. That would be made worse by tying sterling to a Deutschmark that has some way still to rise. West Germany's surplus, due to an undervalued exchange rate used as a protective device, is Europe's problem. The exchange rate is a market-clearing mechanism. That of a country with mass unemployment must be overvalued if any increase in growth leads to a balance-of-payments crisis, which is Britain's situation. That of a country enjoying a balance-of-payments surplus must be undervalued if an increase in growth increases the surplus, as in West Germany. Europe needs an increase in the price of West German goods to make them less competitive and give the rest of Europe a chance to grow. Instead, the EMS requires other currencies to hold down the Deutschmark, harming their economies to allow West Germany to export even more powerfully. That is the major reason why Europe as a whole is growing so slowly, why unemployment is so high and why France and Italy have lost impetus and languish today.

Britain would go into the EMS at too high a rate of exchange that would then be set in aspic to be influenced, if not controlled, by competitors with a vested interest in keeping it high to sustain their access to our market. Every instrument of British policy would be geared to sustaining it, but with our inflation rate higher than West Germany's, interest rates would have to be correspondingly higher. Money would flow in on deposit, making it difficult to hold sterling in its bands and requiring internal deflation. As realignment approached – and it would be more predictable and less frequent than outside the Mechanism – the money flows would be suddenly reversed, seeking safety in West Germany until it was time to come back. The result: ever-rising interest rates and a one-way bet for speculators guaranteed against loss by the central banks. Britain would have abandoned control of its own rate. The aim of all economic measures would be centred on achieving West Germany's low inflation rate to maintain parity. This would break any expansionary government and make Labour's job as impossible as was Mitterand's in France; his expansion had to be choked back in 1982 so that France could stay in the EMS, and M. Delors went off to get his reward in Brussels. The devaluation of sterling would be just as necessary as it is with Britain outside the EMS, but it would be less likely and more difficult. The only possible benefit of joining is to make it easier to hold down the rate after the massive fall that would inevitably follow any change of government. That would sustain competitiveness but would hardly be acceptable to other members, who see the EMS as a device to take power from politicians, not to help other nations.

Wishful thinkers try to get round the EC problem in two contrary directions. Euro-enthusiasts, including refugees from the Alternative Economic Strategy (which once advocated a British seige economy but succumbed in about 1980), argue for a collective European expansion to boost EC economies. This would require a simultaneous conjunction of expansionary governments in the major economies, a total change in West German attitudes or stronger EC institutions, or all three. The fact that such an expansion is impossible is not the Euro-enthusiasts' only error. Like those who advocated the 1985 European Trade Union proposal for a simultaneous increase of 1.5 per cent in national growth rates, they take no notice of the propensity to import. With import penetration twice as high in the UK than in West Germany, the latter would benefit disproportionately from collective expansion, Britain hardly at all. The same would apply with a seige Europe protecting itself from imports. If protection there has to be, it needs to be for Britain alone because our problem is unique. It is not helped by collective measures, particularly when the real threat is EC imports. Yet national action – e.g. any national control over unfair trade, dumping, market saturation or other malpractices – is ruled out totally. Collective European protection is no alternative, merely another way of strengthening West German dominance.

Anti-marketeers, on the other hand, see the EC as a problem, not a solution. Britain would certainly gain by leaving the EC, shedding its burdens of agricultural protection, buying food on the cheapest market (even EC-dumped food), forming natural relationships with food producers and sending them British manufactures in return. In effect, a small ship can navigate to suit its own best interests; in a larger flotilla, its needs are fudged and frustrated, as Britain's have been. Britain imports half as much again from the EC as we export, so it would gain from restoring tariffs. If we restored the Common External Tariff against them, it would be highest in industries that most need protection, such as vehicle and textile manufacturing, and a proper devaluation would allow industries to overleap retaliation, for few EC tariffs exceed 15 per cent. We would continue to trade with the Community but on a fairer basis.

Anti-marketeers are correct in arguing the EC structure does not suit us. We need industrial protection and agricultural free trade, but get the reverse. Membership will never be easy until it is changed, but fundamentals cannot be and we cannot get change without concessions in return. The EC is strong enough to harm and hinder our efforts to reconstruct, but not strong enough to help or to distribute benefits fairly between its component parts. Britain is trapped, unable to back trends towards unity because of the damage this does to a periphery, but unable, either, to do anything else. The EC is trapped, too, unable to progress to the European state that would ensure fairness and give peripheries a good deal because it is built on the wrong foundations. What started out as, and still remains, an agricultural protection society is incapable of satisfactory development. Like trying to build a skyscraper on a cow shed.

Britain would do far better to withdraw, continuing to trade, observing all the harmonization requirements but serving its own interests. In recent decades, advantage has rested with the small economies navigating to suit themselves, not the large blocks. Yet in reality neither extreme can now prevail. Each checks the other, and the end result will be compromise, with Britain getting the worst of all worlds. Withdrawal is economically correct, but politically impossible, though only because Labour has abandoned it. Britain will therefore face its problems in an EC context. Enthusiasm for going further is out, too, because until the basis of membership is adjusted, we lose with every advance in unity.

The only possible compromise, therefore, is to repeal Section 2 of the European Communities Act 1972, which gives European law automatic acceptance in Britain and, in effect, makes it superior to ours. That would create the climate of certainty that investment needs by allowing the British government to decide what European legislation it will accept, and preventing British decisions being struck down in haphazard and unpredictable fashion by British courts. It gives the distance necessary for reconstruction, and the leverage to adjust the terms of the relationship. Our problems with the EC arise because its terms suit us less than they do the other member countries, so we are always negotiating from weakness. The problem is compounded by the fact that our system is based on strict obedience to the law, so we cannot cheat but must always comply, while they can do more of what suits them, at least for limited periods. Nor do we have intermediate institutions like the West German *Lander*, which can mediate and even get away with actions that central government cannot.

The only firm base for expansion would be repeal of Section 2, proclaimed in Labour's manifesto so it can be claimed as a mandate by an incoming government, and then used to extract concessions. That would be far more effective than plunging the country into a renegotiation as futile as the one in 1975, which held up every decision for months, or wasting Parliament's time in a long review of the whole legislative framework, or waiting for the endless process of Euro-change which never get anywhere. Repeal of Section 2 would validate all existing legal provisions while a committee of the Commons decides what to make permanent and what to drop; new regulations and decisions would be accepted as Parliament decides, thus giving reconstruction the firm legal basis it needs. Repeal is a new strength, a redressing of odds, not a withdrawal.

Without economic reconstruction, Britain can make no effective contribution to Europe, except as a whingeing dependant. Repeal, therefore, would put us in a position to decide our own destiny, allowing us to pick what we want from Europe *à la carte*. By doing this, we would be accepting the reality of what has become a two-speed Europe – even a three-speed as Austria and Sweden seek association. It would allow us to choose what we want in the knowledge that we need to rebore our engine if we are to get up to speed. Repeal is also a lever to push for change, particularly an end to the follies of the Common Agricultural Policy, financing food mountains by high prices. The EC needs to move towards contributions geared to national wealth, to devise an effective machinery for redistribution of the social and economic benefits of unity, and to make policies with the aim of expansion, growth and jobs, not just keeping the cow sacred. With the weapon of repeal, we could pressure the EC down all these roads, and help ourselves if it will not go. Britain has been the miserable footdragger because of its inadequate terms of membership, but with the ability to choose, it could accelerate processes that would otherwise take decades. We can get what we want, provided we are armed.

If conflict and tension result from the effort to rebuild, all the cards would be in our hands. The EC cannot force their overpriced food on us or their surplus manufactures. Nor could they send back our budget contribution. The British people might not vote to leave the Community, but would certainly be roused to anger by any EC attempt to prevent a British government doing what they had voted for. A government acting for national strength would be well supported. Flexibility would also resolve the other problem of whether to go further and faster towards unity or to call a halt. We would do what suits us, not be prisoners on a train whose destination is decided by others. The EC is not an adventure in international idealism but a commercial relationship that presently benefits only the other member countries. When we redress this, they will negotiate realistically to retain our membership – and our market. We want a more equal relationship with an institution based on fairness, but domestic action to rebuild cannot wait. A strong British economy is what the rest of the EC should want, and it is what we can give them with greater control over our own destiny. If that ends in us retaining membership for useful purposes but recognizing the reality of a Europe of different speeds, different approaches, different degrees of attachment, that is their responsibility. We will be secure.

Britain stands at a crossroads in its barren marriage to Europe. The pace towards becoming more deeply committed is picking up. Britain can hardly go along with it unless the basic imbalance of the relationship is redressed. Coming out is politically improbable, yet so is rebuilding unless we take the necessary steps. Europe may develop in such a way that it can help us, but this will not happen soon, and not at all unless we push it. Until then, the nation-state is the only framework that has been successful at making the people wealthy and giving them democratic control. That state can be built only on a strong industrial base, the one Britain must rebuild. No nation so far has built up its manufacturing while exposed to the full blast of superior competition in an open market. Building has always come first, to be opened outward later. Britain's dilemma is unique, making its resolution doubly difficult within the EC. Membership is a strait-jacket, reinforcing and compounding decline and making impossible the problems of a nation never clear about its own interests. Decisions on that strait-jacket must be made, particularly since some see it as a lifebelt. The odds are that they will not be.

5

Long to Reign Over Us

Prescribing the policies for economic reconstruction is easy. The difficulty is implementation, for change of policy requires change of government.

The British constitution has none of the safeguards of other systems: written guarantees, power dispersed, the citizen made powerful by rights or information, government checked by separation of powers. None was assumed to be necessary. The all-powerful executive might control the legislature, power might be heavily centralized, but the people could always throw out the governing party. That kept democracy open, government responsive. With that power failing, the elective dictatorship has become an irremovable autocracy. The ruling minority is entrenched by a deadlocked political system. Rousseau said that the English are free only at elections. Thanks to that deadlock, they are not even free then.

The problem arises because the social base of politics is out of kilter with the political superstructure. The base has changed. Parties and the electoral system have become rigid. Parties are the hyphen linking society to the machinery of state, transmitting the imperatives of each to the other. They must represent the divisions in society: linguistic in Belgium; religious in Holland and Northern Ireland; regional in Canada and the United States; social and economic in Britain where class and income are the most fundamental differences. Usually the divisions produce two main parties as the US, Australia, New Zealand, Canada and Britain, though in some, such as West Germany and Ireland, they need coalitions, while in others, such as France, the two-party division is more recent and the presidential system simplifies politics to a choice between left and right. In Sweden, three bourgeois parties ally to fight the dominant Social Democrats, so even multi-party systems tend to work on a two-party basis for purposes of power and government.

Parties are social phenomena – the political outcrop of society, giving political expression and coherence to their sections, bonding and organizing them, picking candidates from them, permeating and being permeated, political flesh of their flesh, blood of their blood. The Tories do that for the classes, Labour for the masses, and if the system is to function properly, each party must do its job for as big a group as it can bring together. Alternation requires evenly balanced parties, so each one must bring the maximum numbers together and reach out to even more to widen the vote.

In a two-class society, that means being central to one class but reaching out to the other. The Tories, with a smaller base, have always had to work harder at the first task than Labour, which has sat on the broader bottom of the pyramid. However, with society becoming more pluralistic and, therefore, more suited to coalition government, Labour must learn techniques that do not come naturally to it but which the Tories have always understood.

Mobilization is easier for a party that represents those higher up the ladder. The upper classes have a cohesion springing from possession, education and position which are not as readily available to the Great Remainder. Conserving a vested interest is easier than preparing for change; defence is easier than attack. The interests to be defended are less diffuse and more directly motivating, and the common conditioning of class is stronger, particularly if it has been bought and paid for by private education. Conservatives are more of a tribe; the other side is a coalition. So the 'haves' do not need strong structures and discipline. Those at the top of the tree – the élites of land, finance, commerce, industry, the professions, the whole panoply of possession – are kept together by common interest and instinct, not rules and resolutions. The skill comes in recruiting widows, orphans and the wider fringes, who identify with those above, to sit on the frontline of privilege.

The alternative has the more difficult task of motivating the less interested, educated, informed and involved. Society's Great Remainder do not have the same strong common bonds as 'the classes', their political expression must bridge greater gaps, without the advantages that wealth, class and instinct offer the Conservatives. Strong structures and more elaborate frameworks are essential. Organization is the invention of the Left and has traditionally taken tougher forms – from the Marxist discipline of the vanguard parties to that great Liberal copy of American parties, Joe Chamberlain's Birmingham Caucus, whose rise was so much deplored in the late 19th century. The Left's organizational ability was imitated by the Right, but it was always a paler, weaker, less-disciplined, shadow, restricted to a service role and function, rather than being, as organization became on the Left, the essence of the party. Conservatives thought of the National Union and Central Office as a domestic servant or handmaiden. Over the years, these became more Jeeves than downstairs maid, but still retained that role.

The Conservative Party is Britain's oldest political entity. It has changed as British élites and their interests have changed, from land to money, from empire to European Community, from industry to finance. It has changed its face from die-hard resistance to Lloyd George's social reforms, through municipally inspired modernization in the 1930s and Macmillan's *noblesse oblige* in the 1950s, to the meaner imperatives of today. Margaret Thatcher presides over a harder, more down-market party but one still recognizably the expression of the 'haves' and their broad interests. Tory MPs are now its Pioneer Corps rather than its élite, but that, too, is appropriate to a more populist age. Each guise has advanced the cause in different times.

The representation of the Great Remainder has been less stable. When the dominant issues were reform, religion and the constitution, the alternative to Tory dominance was the Liberal coalition that brought together the Welsh and Scottish fringes and a manufacturing interest, which was only later prised away on the protection issue with the liberal, reforming, middle class, plus non-conformity, and labour, tendencies. As social and economic issues came to the fore, party divisions crystallized round the class world of 'us' and 'them'. The Liberals could have adjusted by becoming a party of social reform. Lib–Labbery was a strong tradition, the North and the peripheries where Liberalism was dominant were the home of the mass working class, and Lloyd George's redistributive taxation and old age pensions had shown a way of replacing Gladstone's power to mobilize the masses with a new one. The Liberal Party could have shifted its weight on to the left foot but never got the chance. They split. Labour broke through to become the alternative to Toryism and the embodiment of the social and economic interests of the mass working class.

Liberalism had been a loose, polycentric coalition that came together in the National Liberal Federation of city and local élites, and in Parliament. It had as many modes as there were interests and issues to be embraced, and a wide range of MPs and candidates: working class, middle class, on the make, or solidly established, aristocrats and *declasses*. Labour replaced this diversity with one ethos, that of its new core – the working class. In Australia and New Zealand, Labour made the unions. In Britain, they made Labour: providing the money, the candidates, the tone, the issues, attitudes and aspirations, the major part of the membership and structure. Union tentacles ran out into the broad working class, which accepted their leadership because they articulated their economic and social interests. Party, unions and working class spoke the same language.

Realignment ushered in the classical phase of two-party politics, still assumed to be the norm of today even though it, too, has now changed. The two parties had as their bases the different sides of the great social gulf – working versus middle class – and relied on permanent support that had been shaped by two different types of social conditioning. The divisions together encompassed a vast majority of the electorate: in 1951, 97 per cent of the vote went to the two. The two armies inherited their political allegiances from their parents. These were reinforced by the social conditioning of neighbourhood, work, education, newspaper, and they faced each other across the barbed wire in mutual incomprehension. Electoral change came not from any pivotal, frontier class, but from the floating voters, a small, loosely integrated, less informed and involved section. Dissent was personified by the Liberal vote, perhaps

15 per cent of the total, and was expressed only where there were Liberal candidates to vote for; more usually the electorate had to choose between the others. The apathetic – perhaps one-fifth of voters – drifted in and out of abstention: less motivated, less likely to vote.

The electoral system was well calculated to take slight shifts in votes and amplify them, by a cube law, into a bigger shift of seats, to provide the strong government that an imperial power then felt it needed. The 'swing of the pendulum' caused by the floaters or abstentions reflected wider reactions against Labour's reforms or Toryism's failures, producing a feeling that it was 'time for a change'. If Britain lacked checks on the government's power, it could always throw it out. Indeed, some such as Sir Karl Pepper saw this as the main virtue of the system. Democracy was not universal suffrage, rights or safeguards, but the ejector seat.

Yet the strongest executive in the democratic world delivered the lowest rate of economic growth, and the consequence of that failure was an increase in the pace of change. With expectations growing faster than the government's ability to deliver, the Conservatives were thrown out in 1964. Labour came in to 'get Britain moving', a laxative treatment that failed, so that party was thrown out in its turn. A pattern was set: governments came in arousing expectations; they failed, usually changing their own policies as they cast around for solutions; and they were thrown out. The world's most stable democracy had more changes of policy – to and from incomes policy, to and from EEC membership, to and from growth, to and from public spending – and more changes of government than any comparable system. Through the 1960s and 1970s, the party in power in Britain changed four times, and in the US and in West Germany three times (though in West Germany, these were mainly coalition transitions). Australia and New Zealand had two changes, France and Japan none. Changes of policy compounded the problem of economic failure, which in turn brought about changes in government. There was no continuity. Britons had always felt a quiet contempt for less stable nations such as France where governments rose and fell, and for the comic-opera Italians. Yet because of the pattern of failure, the bases of our systems were being eroded.

While the old, broad, mass demands for basic needs – jobs, welfare, security, health care – were better satisfied, new demands proliferated. These were mainly partially or completely non-economic – the environment, a desire to be involved, to know what was going on – or resulted from problems affecting parts of people's lives, not the whole: traffic, neighbourhoods, opportunity, education. Many of them were the sport of pressure groups, not parties; others were a reflection of the fact that an increase in the amount of leisure time and a rising standard of living were allowing people to wear more hats, to become involved in more organizations, activities and demands. A pluralistic society is more difficult to fit into two big buckets. It generates a pressure towards diversity which can be satisfied only by proportional representation allowing established parties to adjust and new parties and political interests to emerge: the Glistrup Protest Party in Denmark, Democrats 68 in Holland, Greens in West Germany and Austria, regional nationalisms. Britain felt the same stirrings but recognized it only in Scotland and Wales where the Nationalist vote was sufficiently concentrated to win seats. Elsewhere, pluralism merged with growing frustration and was detoured into 'fairyland fun' politics. Support for the Liberal 'third party' surged because it provided a safety valve as well as an alternative. The surge was so big because Britain's major parties had failed to deliver the growth and well-being that the electorate expected.

In other countries, rapid growth and economic success formed a basis of satisfaction with institutions and parties. Not so here: both parties failed to deliver. Their vote declined as did their share of the electorate – 75 per cent in 1959 to 55 per cent in 1987. Of those who told pollsters that they identified with a particular party, half identified very strongly in the 1960s, but only one-third felt the same way in the 1980s. Turnout at election time was lower and the protest vote for the third party soon grew to a quarter of the electorate (even more at by-elections). A system that penalized third-party voting produced a much higher third-party vote than in Continental countries where third-party voting produced parliamentary results. The new system striving to be born has struggled out of the womb only at by-elections and in opinion polls.

These changes hit both major parties, but a more basic one affected Labour disproportionately: its class base was disintegrating in a society less dominated by class. Working-class life, instincts and institutions had provided a broad bond for Labour, an alternative world to that of wealth and middle-class individualism. The working class was a protective grouping, with its own attitudes, lifestyle and perceptions, but in the post-war period, this ethos was eroded, its structures weakened, its conditioning undermined by the destruction of neighbour- hoods, the death of the old industries (railways, coal, steel, heavy manufacturing) and the pace of change. Service, white collar, small-scale industries replaced huge mills and factories. Cut adrift and gathered only in smaller firms, workers became more exposed to the media than to each other.

'Working class' was a description less strongly felt, less a lifestyle or a badge of identity, increasingly a mark of relative deprivation. It was not a self-sufficient, defensive world of its own but a less integrated, more deprived fringe of the affluent majority. It was the slow death of this working-class–Labourist ethos which created the vacuum into which a babble of ideologies was poured by those who misguidedly assumed some correlation between working-class and left-wing ideology. There could be no greater mistake. The process ruined Labour.

The social pyramid on whose base Labour had built was swelling in the middle: now it was more a social diamond, with the broad majority higher up. From 1964 to 1983, the numbers of manual workers declined from comprising 47 per cent of the electorate to 34 per cent. The white-collar salariat rose from 18 per cent to 27 per cent. Home ownership across all social classes increased from 42 per cent to 62 per cent and even more dramatically among manual workers. This new majority could be called the 'new working class' or even the 'new middle' but they were not a class so much as an amorph-

ous mass that had adopted the lifestyle of the car and home-
owning, Sainsbury-shopping, Habitat-thinking, DIY-doing,
credit-consuming broad middle. Consumers rather than class
components, the differences between the two were economic
rather than class.

The working class, led by its aristocracy, the skilled workers,
had had interests and attitudes in common. In the new society,
the skilled aristocracy of labour identified upwards and began
to see the sub-class below as a threat to their own aspirations,
an inconvenient nuisance rather than allies in the broad advance to power of the working class. In 1987, 34 per cent of
skilled workers voted Labour, 43 per cent voted Conservative.
There had been broad needs in common: education, health,
employment. Now public spending was being seen not as a
universal benefit but a sectional one, supporting public-sector
workers, scroungers and those who would not provide for
themselves. As the tax burden shifted down from the middle
class this was even more resented by the skilled industrial
worker who had to pay for it. Labour compounded the problem by devising an incomes policy that hit the skilled and
better paid the hardest. In Sweden, social solidarity between
the high- and low-paid produced benefits for both. Here, it
was used negatively to cope with the problems of failure.

As the old working class split, its disintegrating sections
drew apart from the concerned middle-class individuals who
formed a considerable proportion of Labour's army. With
economic issues as the battleground, there was little to divide
them from the workers who wanted a fairer society achieved
by better public spending, for the middle class took most of the
benefits. Yet the middle-class Labour supporters were also
more liberal, humanitarian, radical and tender-minded than
the working class, who tended to be more authoritarian,
tough-minded, conservative. On hanging, corporal punishment, crime, racial issues, sexual matters and abortion,
Labour's enlightened attitudes were broadly in tune with its
middle-class supporters, but out of sympathy with the old working class and their offspring in the new middle. So a gulf
opened up, widening as new issues became more salient and
the old unifying ones faded.

*

The result of all these changes is a new electorate, melding with the old one as it fades. Sustained conditioned allegiances remain, but they now motivate less than half the electorate where they once moved the majority. The rest choose as political consumers, not through a conditioned reflex that has only to be triggered. The parties no longer influence them directly. The real influences are the sedimentation of impressions – the fall-out from the media, particularly television, which have the direct input that the parties, deprived of the conditioned links, now lack. The media are the new gatekeepers and instigators because they deluge the public with information and images that people are less able to fit into a framework of beliefs and attitudes. Minds now resemble a littered street, no longer a collection of stamps neatly mounted into a party album. Parties have become an external, no longer the political outcrop of the social-conditioning process; they compete for attention.

All of this changes the game. Weaker party loyalties are paralleled by weaker brand loyalties in the product market, weaker domestic loyalties in marriage and weaker channel loyalties (and, as in politics, a weaker inheritance factor) in television. In the latter, what was once a secure audience has now become more capricious and less predictable. It has to be won, worked for, lured with sensation and attention-grabbing programmes, beguiled with more diversity from our broadcasting organizations. So, too, in politics. Parties must sell themselves, not rely on a Pavlovian conditioned reflex. They live or die by the impressions they make yet are unable to control either the source or their impact. Being in a political market, they must appeal to consumers but are unable to manipulate them to quite the extent that companies can build demand by advertising. Nor can they explain to consumers who are confused, subject to a welter of impressions but less capable of making sense of them, ordering them, coping with them. In the main, they are able to reach people directly only through the media, the enemies of explanation. They are driven remorselessly downmarket. In a world of intensifying competition, who can keep their scruples, dignity or knickers when all around are losing theirs?

The Conservatives are better placed to sell in this consumer market. Leadership dominance and tribal instincts sustain impressions of unity and competence. Instincts come over better than ideology, particularly when expressed in the populist simplicities of Margaret Thatcher, who has a genius for putting what she does not understand into language that everyone can follow. Tories are at home with markets and marketing, and are more ready to give professionals their heads than a party that thinks it knows what the people want without having to hear it from them. The Tories have but one principle: to win. Labour has more scruples, and dislikes compromise with the electorate; conning the voters is the Conservative approach. That party was just as divided as Labour but far more ready to work with any available grain to conserve what it had: generalizing where Labour was too specific; bland where Labour was prone to *mea culpa*s. Labour, like the British car industry, was more concerned with engineering the product than selling it, and unprepared to do what failing producers must – that is, rethink both product and sales strategy – because thought had become alien, driven out by slogans. For Labour, sales, communications, image building were not essentials that no party can do without, but more footballs in an internal argument that was itself all-absorbing.

As well as these initial advantages, the Conservatives also learned quickly how to cope with the new world, mainly by changing the product. They were being Tebbitized, a process of which Margaret Thatcher was symptom and beneficiary but not cause. Increasingly, the Tories spoke in the new populist language appropriate to reaching people pried loose from previously secure anchorages. They emphasized tax cuts, home ownership and law and order – issues that stirred the masses. As the party went downmarket for its candidates, it did even better, for though the 'angels in the marble' of the deferential working class had once voted for a class born to rule, Conservatism now attracted greedier aspirants as a party born to grab, offering selfishness and self-interest and winning ever more working-class votes. It still spoke for those who have, but in an affluent society when an increasing number felt they had a bit more and wanted more, Mrs Thatcher's party of self-made men and women who worship their creator was less alien than the old upper-class party, and less so, too, than the university lecturers preaching at them on the Labour side. There was no longer any need for voters to feel in awe of the Tories who, after all, were now dominated by people who seemed much the same as themselves, undistinguished by cachet, accent or culture. Not people to look up to, just another part of the same greedy conspiracy.

Those opposed to the Tory incumbency were becoming ever more diverse and divided, a collection of the alienated, not an army. Labour, however, still treated them as if they were the old working class, mobilized in the unions, speaking the old language. Unfortunately, the party never updated its vocabulary so what it said came out as awkward and unreal. Many of those who spoke were a generation removed from the working class, asserting their Labour identity by maintaining the deep frozen postures of its past, at a time when the party really needed a broader, more diffuse congregation, less preoccupied with class basics and more concerned with common ground, but no new Gladstone came along to proclaim a new mobilizing principle for the anti-Tory coalition. If only Labour had moved with the times, as the French Socialists did, to a new, broader coalition, social change need not have been a fatal blow and Labour could have become a looser, less monolithic party as the Liberals had been and the American Democrats still are. Instead, it rigidified in its old mould, trying harder to become what it had once been, when it needed to be very different. The product was not to be changed.

Less in tune with its natural electorate, Labour was no longer at the centre of the world it had to win. It had become a part, not the whole, of the left-of-centre world, in a universe visibly moving the other way. Electorates do not inevitably vote for selfishness as other bonds weaken, but rather lapse into it because no alternative is offered. Labour hardened in its less attractive characteristics rather than updating its evangel. It needed a wider range of more attractive candidates to represent wider ranges of opinion, but lost many in the 1981 split and excluded others by re-selection, preferring stock types from Central Casting: 'working class' lads sprung from it but no longer of it, defiantly suing anyone who denied a background they wore proudly as an identity. This compounded a growing problem, for the loss of rural and town seats had already turned Labour into a big-city party, rather than one of all the people. Labour needs a wide range of candidates and councillors: people running small businesses, professionals, the media glossies, women (particularly career women), environmentalists, more (but genuine) workers, reformers, advertising and PR people, financiers – those who have made something of themselves (rather than climbed union and party hierarchies), few of whom can recite Clause 4 backwards, all of whom find selection difficult now. At present, an increasingly diverse electorate is presented with the typecast candidates that the party wants, not those the electorate might prefer. Labour has not seen that Harry Perkins is fiction.

Labour continued to talk in class and union terms when it needed to be classless, exploring new issues, taking up the problems of all people and shifting to a broad populist appeal. In its puzzlement, it attempted to buy groups. The result was disaster, for people do not function as group members but as individuals and must be won over on the issues that matter to them. The language of the mass is populism, not sectionalism.

The consequences of these social changes and Labour's failure to adjust to them are a weakened party system. It is less now an evenly balanced two-party system than one in which the Conservatives are dominant, Labour is an under-party and the third party works on a different dimension entirely. This one-and-two-thirds alternative entrenches the dominant party like the Liberal Democrats in Japan, the Social Democrats in Sweden, the Right in France up to the 1980s, a period ended only by the transformation of the French Socialists. Britain's situation is similar, but our 'first past the post' system excludes the minority and throws disproportionate power to the biggest party, virtually handing it the elective dictatorship. The forms and rituals of the old party game go on, but the Tories are dominant, and the opposition is unable to challenge or check the onward progress of folly because it offers reduced prospects of power. Britain's politics are now as exciting as predestination. The old two-party pattern – Tories creating pre-election booms as in 1963 and 1973, Labour cleaning up the mess – has been broken. Nigel Lawson is the first chancellor to have to change his nappy where other nations change governments.

'Time for change' will be strong by the next election, though in judging its impact, the analyst is driven to abnormal psychology rather than psephology. So much depends on Margaret Thatcher. Even her infinite variety might begin to stale, her rejuvenation tire, and if she hits reality with her handbag enough times, it will eventually hit back. A government as dominated as this one will build up explosive pressures – resentments, blighted hopes, frustrated prospects – that could lead to more cases of Heseltine psychosis, even a political Jonestown, and with more electors open to change, the potential for it grows, though the Democrats, too, could rise with that tide. All the while, Labour could be reforming, improving, looking more impressive and getting itself into shape. As the political weatherhouse turns, Labour would then not be seen to put a foot wrong because it would have the charisma of the peoples' anointed, where for years it has hardly been allowed to put one right, under the aura of failure. The Democrats are the wild card here, too.

All possible, some probable. The government looked better from 1986 to 1989 than it should have or ever will again, and with the 1959–64 Parliament being paralleled very closely, there is no reason why the government's standing should not now collapse like a soufflé, as it did then. Yet despite all its scandals and problems, much of the Tories' support had returned by 1964 when a frenetic media and a confident electorate favoured change. Now, seeming stability, dulled interest and a more nervous nation strengthen the incumbent, particularly when the latter can avoid suicide and scandal, massage the media and run the economy with more attention to the polls than M3. With or without Margaret Thatcher, this government is not going to forget the tricks it learned in 1983 and 1987. All can be dusted down and reused, albeit with diminished effect, in 1991. A majority of 100 can endure two normal swings, even one massive one, and has a longer lease on life than any predecessor.

The majority in seats is the same as that of the Macmillan

government in 1959, swept away in 1964. Yet in votes, Macmillan's majority was 4 per cent over Labour; Margaret Thatcher's is 12 per cent. Labour needs a swing of 6 per cent just to displace the Tories from power and become the largest single party. It needs 8 per cent for a bare majority. The largest swing since 1945 has been 5 per cent. Electors are usually kinder to Conservatives. With the country in turmoil, a three-day week and a government determined on suicide, Edward Heath suffered an adverse swing of only 2 per cent in 1974. What price, then, a government that has managed the news and manipulated opinion while merely wasting opportunities and gambling away the nation's future?

Nor does an examination of Britain's history offer much hope. Periods of political transition have always been times of one-party dominance, entrenching the dominant party in power. The changes then were in political parties rather than in society, but the effect was the same because the balance between parties is decisive. For example, when the Conservatives split over the repeal of the Corn Laws, the Peelites went their own way to merge eventually with the Liberals, while during a long period of opposition the protectionists rebuilt themselves into what we now know as the Conservatives. The result was two decades of 'Whig–Liberal' governments. The same happened in the inter-war period. The rise of Labour after the split in the Liberal party in 1918 produced two decades of Conservative government, with minority Labour interludes.

Transitions entrench one party because of Britain's electoral system: division on one side splits the vote and gives a minority on the other more seats than it would otherwise get. The 'winner takes all' political system then gives that party total power. The same forces operate today. The same consequence now means two decades of bankrupt Tory government while opposition is divided and the economic situation just disintegrates. Even now there is no guarantee of a new balance. Labour is not going to die as the Liberals did before their second coming, nor is there a political law that says dominant parties must slip back, or under-parties become political Charles Atlases. Nor are the pressures towards third-party escapism going to vanish. Indeed, though they have damaged themselves, the Democrats would almost certainly have won the Epping and Richmond by-elections had David Owen's game of Kamikaze 'chicken' not divided the protest vote and held them back in the polls. These are the politics of futility but the only way in which the present system can adjust — unless, that is, parties work together to counter its imperatives.

A change of electoral system offers more relevant ways forward by giving influence to parties in transition and tempering the power of the majority. In proportional representation, a minority party cannot dominate. Parties are pushed into coalition, and in such a situation, few would throw down their capes for Queen Margaret. There is less power to take, fewer outright winners. Indeed, in Austria, civil war between 'black' and 'red' produced a determination to work together which was written into the constitution. All the parties above a certain level of representation must be in the governments of the nine provinces, and now there is a coalition at the centre, too. In Finland, the balance of power produced the same result. The two majors worked together in the 1960s, and even now, the power of the winner is diluted by partners.

Similarly, in federal systems a party displaced at the centre has bases elsewhere: Democrats control most of the state governorships and the Congress in the United States, where there is a Republican executive; in West Germany, the SPD has firm bases in the *Lander*. Other legislatures disperse the power we concentrate on the governing party. In Sweden, the three Bourgeois parties share power through parliamentary committees, and there is a requirement to get agreement before any action can be taken. Nowhere else in the democratic world can the winner monopolize all the power, still less use it to destroy the bases of its opponents.

Any of these approaches would help. In combination, they would loosen Britain's rigidities and break our deadlock. Unfortunately, we operate with a constitution that perpetuates our problems. Since institutions compound these, the onus for breaking the political stalemate lies with the opposition. It must provide the viable alternative that people need if they are to feel able to turn out the government. One party must broaden its reach to build viability, or two parties must work together, or both. Change in the system is impossible without a prior change of government. That is impossible without a viable alternative. The system cannot change unless the opposition does. Labour is the key.

6
Escaping the Trap

Prophecies of doom should have a remorseless inevitability. After a decade, the Conservatives appear immovable. After its re-election, the government remained further ahead in the polls and for longer than any predecessor, Labour languishing behind in the upper 30s when it needed to be in the upper 40s, 10 per cent behind when it could not win even if it were 10 per cent ahead at that stage of the game. Although the belated turn around began in early 1989, opposition remained divided, the government's support still strong. Nevertheless, the basic rule of politics is that there are no rules in politics. Nothing is inevitable. The Thatcherite hegemony is not impregnable. The Prime Minister won power by accident, came near to losing it over Westland and, despite all the propaganda to the contrary, remains mortal. More electors are open to change, the unexpected usually happens, a radical, wrongheaded government must do more to precipitate change than any predecessor, and the fear and loathing focused at the court of the Queen-Empress could always burst apart.

So hope springs eternal. Only the odds argue, weightily, against change. Labour has to mobilize every weapon and change drastically to have any prospect. The Labour party of 1974–9, a mixture of corporate state and duty, only just won then and cannot again. Nor could the Labour Party of 1979–83, so badly damaged at its own hands that it was incapable of winning anything. The much better party of 1984–7, pulling itself up but not far enough, changed but insufficiently, was better but nowhere near well enough. It did not make it then and may not later, even when it has shed more incubuses. The only Labour Party that can win is one that enthusiastically embraces the new politics and the new electorate by reaching out to the whole nation, not just to its chosen people. The best way of demonstrating to a doubting population the scale and sincerity of its conversion is by being open to new approaches and relationships.

These are huge changes for a party as conservative as Labour, and perhaps impossible ones for a party where power rests with those whose influence must be diluted. Nor does change guarantee victory. It can boost other trends: the weather-house effect; the growing concern about the crumbling country; the failure of both markets and government. All consummations devoutly to be wished, but far from inevitable and uncertain in their electoral impact, even with a changed Labour Party. There are many prescriptions for change, but no clear route to success. The party must be made anew but relevant. There is no guarantee even of that.

Labour is the key to the deadlock as well as the central problem of British politics. If it changes, the system can. If it does not, deadlock is sustained, the hegemony of failure perpetuated. Partial change has begun but has not gone far enough because Labour's vision is circumscribed by its own narrow bounds, its dilemma viewed in party terms. The new age is one of less-than-party politics and wider-than-party appeals. So in a less-than-three-but-more-than-two-party system, the rules require Labour not only to fight the Tories but to displace the third party, a confusing situation for traditionalists and both difficult transitions for a conservative party to make.

This is why Labour's situation must be understood in its full starkness – not to reinforce the psychology of defeat which has crept over the party, but to demonstrate that Labour cannot buck the laws of political science as it attempted after 1979 or even continue to work by its old rules. Both mean relegation to a sectional party. Failure to understand reality has compounded Labour's problems, its own irresponsibly, the nation's disastrously. Atonement is never easy. It can be humiliating, but Labour is the only chance – and that slim – of breaking the mould. Change is essential for its sake and the nation's.

Labour combines suspicion of the 'meejah' with fear, where it should use them. It looks to the triumphal march of the faithful. In fact, it is in a market, and parties are sales organizations not crusades. It speaks to unionists and workers where it should speak to all the people, not just the annointed few, and must persuade them, not treat electors like Pavlov's dogs. The Conservatives, as masters of the art of conning wider numbers to support structures of wealth and power which are not in their interest, quickly learned these lessons. Labour did not because it saw its job as selling pure principles. Its decline is as much due to that as to any irreversible social change. Led by the best saleslady in the land, the Tories peddled populism and images instead of policy, reached out to mobilize every discontent in every heart and offered a simple prospectus in which it promised to do better without saying how. Labour doggedly did its duty, and was hurt and disorientated when chucked out for it. Recovery now requires an end to Labour's constant prostration before the classes and interests that it already represents: the poor, CND, the women's lobby, the traditional working class, the unions and all the other friends who failed us in the crisis. Take them for granted and go out to face a new world that is none of those things. Talk to that world in its language, not ours.

The Conservative Party is geared to seize every opportunity; it is a machine for winning. Labour's machine is a full-time distraction. The structure makes a mockery of Labour values: fraternity, because we show none to each other; equality, because block votes belie it and we compete savagely to rise; liberty and democracy, because our structure provides neither; and cooperation, because we show none. The constitution dates from 1918, our political ethos and attitudes from the 1930s, our electoral approach from the 1950s: all brilliantly designed for a world that is dead. The theory is that organized Labour transmits conditioned reflexes to a committed vote, while the machine gives power to members, not people, because activists lead, people follow. Unfortunately, none of it works, and much of it is counter-productive. The only solution is to change it. Imitate success and accept the 1980s, even as they become the 1990s.

Three decades ago, Harold Wilson called Labour 'a penny farthing in the jet age'. It is now in the space age but its back wheel has fallen off. Rather than a mass party without members, an ideological crusade without an agreed ideology, a peoples' party cut off from the people, it must become a broad, diffuse, looser coalition for change, mobilizing more, demanding less – a sales organization selling to political consumers, a rally rather than a party. Images, impulses and a sense of movement are more important than policy; PR and market research more necessary than providing an adventure playground for the ideologically motivated. Taking what the people want and amplifying it back to them, blended with a party's own values, is a more useful technique than the continuous creation of policies. People are more important than members. A less demanding, more offering party is a voice for values rather than a policy factory of theorists immersed in an all-absorbing, perpetual, policy process. For the Labour Party, politics is something that happens while we are making policy. It should be everything.

A loose *rassemblement* or a popular front is more appropriate to consumer politics where brand loyalty has to be boosted by attraction to impulse buys. A DIY *Tod und Verklarung* might do the job – failing that, a total overhaul. Unfortunately, this is even more difficult in a conservative party that is becoming arthritic. Aspiring to internal democracy with undemocratic structures, wanting more power for the activists when there are fewer of them, aiming for mass membership at a time of mass leisure, and needing change where vested interests block it, Labour is trapped. It pulls levers that no longer work, then pulls them more vigorously, rather than face up to the fact that it must become a different party and pull different levers. It finds change difficult because it cannot look outside itself, but inside, power is controlled by those who benefit from the status quo.

Socialism is an opposition mentality only here. Elsewhere it rules because our counterparts overseas are parties of government, getting power, using it to build new support and to change their approach and appeal. In Britain, the Labour Party has used power to cut the living standards of its supporters, while its members, frustrated at that failure, became opposition minded, seeing the party, not as an incumbent in the system or a machine for power, but as a party of socialism.

To them, Labour does not fail when it fails to win, only when it betrays socialism. The party is readier to assert principles in their purity than defile them with power. Rather than show itself competent at running the system, it prefers to be pure in thought , word and deed. It matters not who won or lost, but how they served the cause of socialism. The electorate's reaction is different. If Labour can't run itself, how can it run the country?

Such conditioned attitudes made the futile follies of 1978–83 inevitable. Instead of modernizing to win, the party embarked on its Great Lurch Backwards, a reaction against the Labour government of 1974–9. That government had not won power; it had just been better at not losing elections than Edward Heath. Without a majority and facing the most severe economic crisis since the war, Labour brought the country through and did a far better job than in 1964–70 when, with a majority sufficient to do anything, it couldn't think of much to do with it. Yet to party members, stopping the stone from rolling backwards was seen as failure. They wanted it rolled forward, equality advanced, the better society built and all preferably overnight, by Resolutionary Socialism. The government had betrayed them. Organizational reforms to bind the party to socialism would stop it doing so again.

Conceived in the 1970s and implemented in the 1980s, this activists' agenda would never have got off the ground had not Labour's guardian angels averted their attention. Alienated by the prolongation of the incomes policy and by James Callaghan's failure to call an election in October 1978, the trade unions abandoned their custodial role as the security staff in Labour's mental hospital and allowed the bum's rush into folly. Re-selection ensured that Members of Parliament and candidates were pure, if not attractive, becoming more uniform while those of other socialist parties were becoming more diverse. A cumbersome electoral college ensured suitably socialist leaders who could be called to account, and made appeal to the party paramount. Conference control of the manifesto was urged to ensure that it suited the activists. This failed but a radical programme of fundamentalist conference commitments was published in *Labour's Programme*, followed by Lunacy's Greatest Hits, a draft manifesto drawn up by the NEC without the usual consultative processes that require the manifesto to be agreed between NEC and PLP. 'The longest suicide note in history' was one cynic's appropriate description.

The intention was to boost working-class support. In practice, it tested Labour's incumbency in the two-party system almost to destruction. Mrs Thatcher's honeymoon had been the shortest in history; the opposition was quickly ahead in the polls. The people wanted a return to the acceptable and familiar, which was the Callaghan Labour Party, but as they began to say, 'Come back, Jim, all is forgiven,' they were offered a civil war masquerading as a political party, an anti-leader-leader, an uncertain and frightening prospect. The poll lead vanished.

If a government moves in an extreme direction, the logic of the two-party system requires the opposition to occupy the centre ground – that amorphous area of confused attitudes, contradictory feelings and vague good intentions where most people live. There, it is in the only position to win. Instead, responding to socialist imperatives rather than political sense, Labour countered the government's move to the extreme by moving to its own, opposite, extreme and into exile.

The people disliked the policies and feared a move to the left that was loudly exaggerated by the media. Labour appeared – because it was – divided, incapable of doing its job, dominated by sinister forces and deeply unattractive. It was also split. Those who defected – the Gang of Four, over a score of MPs, plus party members up and down the country – gave credence to the tale of the 'great shift left' and boosted the Liberals. Labour plummeted. The Alliance surged. Four years in the death of the Labour Party became the prelude to a disastrous 1983 election defeat, with Labour 2 per cent ahead of the Alliance in Britain, and only 0.5 per cent ahead in England. The government was given (for it hardly had to win) a majority of 120 over all other parties.

At that nadir, Neil Kinnock took over the leadership. He saw that the party had to move back to the centre, mobilize the arts of public relations and media management, sidetrack the left into irrelevance, dump the unsaleable and build a new unity. As a man of his party, playing by its rules, conditioned by its structures and attitudes, he did all that democratically, which meant slowly, rather than pointing to reality and leading from the front. He devoted more time and effort to the party than to the world. The damage proved to be too deep, the loss of attractive figures and a vital strand of support too grievous and too recent, and the leader had to tread too gingerly. Labour was bemused, rather than enthusiastically and clear-headedly saluting the new agenda. So progress was slow. The aim should have been quick, dramatic action achieved by an assertion of leadership, and a simple, moderate policy concentrating on basic values. Labour's structures and inertias precluded this.

Labour could not have won the 1987 election. It was not fully trusted. It did not exude competence. The Tory government had caused neither the necessary alienation nor the feeling that it was time for change; those in work were becoming better off. The real need was to win back enough seats and support to get power next time, and to roll back the Alliance. It succeeded at neither. The Labour vote rose by 3 per cent. The Alliance vote fell, but by only 2 per cent, remaining high at 23 per cent, 5 per cent up on 1974. With 31 per cent of the vote, Labour won 229 seats, an increase of only a score. The Pilgrimage of Grace was going to take longer than had been assumed by those who had hoped that a quick respray and a modern communications glass would be enough. The advertising was better than the product.

The government is as strong as the opposition is weak, and the latter's stature depends on its prospects. On that test, Margaret Thatcher can get away with anything and is still doing so. The system is at a stalemate because everything is 'not quite'. Labour is the opposition but not quite the alternative, not quite commanding popular support, and not quite poised to win next time. The Democrats have again raised their aim from winning the balance of power to displacing Labour as the incumbent alternative, yet they are unable to do either. Except at by-elections, the 'not quite' elections. The government is triumphant, but not quite popular, not quite a majority. It is exposed, as all governments are, to the normal process of rejection, but not quite, for a majority of 102 is a good basis from which to ride it out. It does not even have to win, just not quite lose. The whole situation is not quite a basis for decisive change, more for muddled confusion, frustration and blighted hopes.

The one thing that is more than 'not quite' is Labour's position as the central problem. The government has failed but cannot be turned out because Labour is not yet an inevitable alternative, poised to win and operate the levers of change. Unlikely to reach power on its own, neither will it cooperate with anyone else. It cannot change and grow because its constitution roots it to the past, and its balance of forces requires change to be carried through by those who must lose by it. Yet it cannot form new coalitions either for the same reasons. Labour must save itself. Until it does, Britain cannot be saved.

Oppositions do not win, governments lose. This government is beginning to fulfil its part of the bargain. However, consumer politics are not merely those of the pendulum swing, and the maxim does not give the opposition the licence merely to sit there waiting. It must present itself in the most attractive light to win the support that the government loses. It must not alienate or annoy. It must broaden appeal and approach, serving wider interests, offering success rather than protection. All necessary but not necessarily enough, for now, as Labour waits with its surfboard ready, it has a competitor for the tide.

Still, Labour is poised for its chance: better organized, more serious, more competent, with an impressive front-bench team and a passionate, caring leader. It has not been in such good shape since 1974. Change is in the air. A wilful government of neurotic drives rather than considered strategies is going to create a bigger backwash of hostility than previous 'do nothing and ask your grandmother' Conservative governments. Yet will the tide of change carry Labour to power? In 1964, despite a substantial swing, Labour achieved a majority of two. In 1974, it was merely the largest single party. Project that declining curve forward to 1991 and it means failure. So Labour must change dramatically, and opt for bold leadership, not make-do-and-mend. Yet improvement removes the incentive for change. As the government's fortunes decline, the alteration of mood could breed over-confidence, a feeling that all that is necessary has been done. In fact, the rise in the polls will be fool's gold, the inter-election slump from which all governments suffer, and most rally – particularly Tories.

Labour must work by the rules of party competition and political markets, not those of socialism. It carries a greater responsibility than any opposition has before. Unless Labour is changed, the government cannot be. Party is about power, Labour about socialism. The two do not mix. Rather than concentrating on its real job of getting power and using it for its people, Labour sees itself as the political arm of the Great Movement of Labour, a self-appointed role that is a full-time job in its own right and not much to do with a party's real function: winning power to serve the people.

The Tory Party allows itself no such luxuries. It serves the Leader, and the Leader is there to win power. Otherwise a knife in the back, a body in the river. Any deity is dropped from the Tory pantheon as soon as market research shows that it is becoming dated: Empire, Paternalism, Affluence, Butskellism, Keynes, Euro-Enthusiasm – all are now in the Central Office junk room. Tories gear their appeal to the times and the mood, and their party to power. Nothing is allowed to stand in the way: taste (given their Yobbo appeal), loyalty, consistency, honesty, certainly not conservatism (given their radical policies). They cultivate any new approach as it comes off the American test benches, or as soon as their pollsters tell them the public want it.

Even though Labour finds all this distasteful, imitation would be effective. Until Labour is as crude and direct and as obsessed with the essentials of power and 'people manipulation' as the Tories, it will not be doing its job, for none of this is a betrayal of principle, merely a way of furthering it. Sadly, the world has changed, not the party. There is now no mass working class, no automatically conditioned loyalties or mass causes: Life is more home-centred and privatized, society more pluralistic, class feelings weaker, basic demands more satiate, others more numerous and complex. Electors are consumers and have choice. Parties have to sell. Politics is more a question of mood creation and reality management than lectures and shopping lists.

Tories have done better. Labour has failed, neither countering Mrs Thatcher's populism nor substituting its own sales formula. It has hardly sought new channels, merely behaved more moderately in the existing ones. Uncertain how to get through, what language to talk, which chords to strike, it turns inward for reassurance, pulling the comforts of the past and the loyalties of the irrelevant round itself for warmth.

Labour's structure is counter-productive in the new media politics. Coalitions argue and discuss, but that comes over as disunity. The Tories, a leadership party and a tribe, present a bland, confident face. Labour is ideological, the Tories a party of instincts, which are more saleable and understandable. Labour is poor, working class, associated with trade unions (which, as mass organizations, will never be popular however effective they become). It is dominated by the yapping professions who talk at people. The Tories, being richer, are more professional. They have developed a more polished appeal, and benefit from all sorts of supplementary access points to boost the messages coming from the television screen: a press that is overwhelmingly Tory; more money to spend on advertising: the 'non-political' publications; the pronouncements of business executives, authority, élites generally. They have even gone downmarket to suit candidate to constituency, while the main legacy of 1979–83 is that Labour made its candidates more uniform, all eager to live down to a 'working class' lifestyle which lives only in their imagination. Labour needs a wider range of candidates to suit candidate to seat not impose the same stereotype everywhere.

Mass membership and unions are supposed to be Labour's tentacles to reach out to the world. In fact, membership is small, under 300,000, and unlikely to get back to the 1 million target in a satiate, well-entertained society. Political commitment is now almost as isolating as leprosy, and lepers can neither relay the mood and views of the people back to the party, nor educate the people to the party's policies. Instead, they huddle together, refugees from the world rather than Labour's ambassadors to it. The more the Parliamentary Labour Party listens to party activists, the less it hears the community. The more influence activists get, the less the people have. The influence of members should be proportionate to their contribution to victory. It is pointless to concede control over policy to a membership as small as ours, particularly if the party then has to devote time and effort to frustrating their wishes, navigating round their follies and generally fudging and mudging, making the resulting, unacceptable policies incomprehensible to minimize damage.

Labour also needs a new policy settlement with the unions. Some of them, particularly the EEPTU and the GMB, have changed more successfully than Labour itself, having grasped the need to serve their members. Yet union policy processes are still not adequate, and a dependence on unions to frustrate the follies of its rank and file gives Labour the image of being union-dominated. More sensible would be to deal directly with the unions on policy, rather than amplify their inadequacies by integrating their policy structure into ours. On industrial issues, the apathy and lack of involvement of members can fairly be taken as approval, for if they did not like what has been done, they would leave. Matters of politics are more peripheral to them so this rule of inertia does not apply. However, this leaves the unrepresentative few to take political decisions in the name of the many, decisions that, because members are not interested enough to bother, are not then protested or controlled in the way that unions would be. Unions thus end up taking positions that represent the activists, not the members and certainly not the public, a process of which the TGWU is a past master, building houses of policy cards with no bases. Therefore, the unions' contributions to decisions on the electoral college, re-selection, nationalization, union power, policy disputes, nuclear disarmament, even leadership votes bias the party in wrong directions and bring it into disrepute with the wider public – particularly when such measures are imposed by union block votes.

Labour has a warm, bleeding heart. Its members are the salt of the earth, concerned people who want to improve the lot of humanity. Its social side, its conferences, its tribal meetings are as heart-warming as they are disorganized. Its passion and concern, its continuity with the great past and the noble mission of Labour are deeply moving. It needs a professional backbone and an efficient approach to make a voluntary organization work in an age of political apathy, but instead it can be an infuriating shambles, resistant to change and particularly inept at policy formulation. The machine has become a full-time preoccupation, not an aid to power. Where Sisyphus made three steps forward for every two he fell back, Labour at times averages two for two because every gain seems to be promptly followed by a loss, every triumph by a folly. Political parties should have a higher purpose than DIY existentialism.

Labour's machine also encourages internal argument by providing an alternative power structure for dissidents. In power there is a constituency for opposition to government's actions. Out of it, the left further their careers by telling fools what they want to hear, rather than exposing them to reality. In no other party could those who are least attractive to the public come so regularly at the top of the popularity stakes. Labour says that it desires a genuine mass membership, but it has the attitudes of a clique.

Reform must be directed towards allowing the party to do its job by making it flexible, permeable, open to the world, extending Labour's tentacles out into society so it can embrace everyone and become a channel for two-way communication. Party is a service agency to power and should not pretend to control the exercise of power. Make it advisory on policy, not dominant; give it consultation in leadership matters, not control; let it devote its time and effort to making the machine work effectively, not telling the leadership how to run the world.

Conference should be a showplace for the party – not a parliament but a sounding board, an adult education class, with some particularly recalcitrant pupils. Hand responsibility down to regional conferences. Make the NEC a management team, not a politbureau. Labour cannot afford the luxury of an alternative power structure for those who don't make it in the real world or a court of appeal for the disgruntled in the PLP; leading figures should not have to divert time needed for talking to the nation because the party is deaf or because their votes are needed to sustain fragile majorities. Keep Parliamentarians out of the party's internal politics and positions, except as representatives of the PLP, and bring parliamentary and extra-parliamentary frameworks together only in joint meetings. Recognize the subordinate role of the party outside Parliament: not a handmaiden but a workmate.

Instead of tackling reform as a matter of urgency, Labour tinkers rather than grasping the central purpose. It opted for the confusing folly of local electoral colleges, for candidate selection instead of one person one vote. In particular, it went for a half-baked compromise on cheaper membership fees by keeping them too high so it still turns membership into a self-perpetuating clique, but adding a reduced fee of £5.00 for members of affiliated unions to the £3.00 already paid by pensioners and students. It got the worst of all worlds, becoming more union-dependent but doing little to recruit on a mass basis to change the complexion of the membership as a whole.

Labour must persuade the larger, looser fringe, which registers for parties in the United States and in whose name party committees then act, to enrol if not join by establishing a system of loose contacts so the party can reach further out into society. The answer is a two-tier memebership: £5.00 to be paid by those keen to take an active role: a show commitment, £1.00, a flag day donation, from 'associate members', mostly electors canvassed as 'pro'. Then mailing lists central and local can be built up to get direct debit donations and send out a regular supply of information, letters from the relevant MP or candidate, and 'fact pieces' to provide ammunition and give people an alternative to a biased media. All members should have the opportunity to participate democratically, by postal ballot, in all the party's functions. This would include policy, leadership and the selection of candidates and MPs by mass primaries coupled with postal balloting. Throwing selection open to greatly increased numbers will widen the range of choice, give more power to women, and make personality, attractiveness and suitability to the seat more important than party duty. Labour is in danger of becoming a social sealed knot: descendants of the working class fighting, the battles of a generation back which the rest of society has given up on. Nothing wrong with the type, unless it is all the party offers. However, a wider range of candidates, drawn from all sections of society and with a wider spread of opinions, will make Labour more attractive.

Under this proposed membership system, some members will graduate up the ladder to the £5.00 rate, and this income would be supplemented by regular donations to 'giving schemes' managed by Walworth Road using its centralized computerized records. The local party could keep the associate membership fees as an incentive to widen Labour's net, with Walworth Road depending on the full members' fees, union money donated nationally and what it can raise by lotteries, giving schemes, mail order, festivals, tours, advertising and all the other market-orientated activities that can be devised to pay the wages of its staff and those of a force of agents and professionals, the backbone a voluntary party needs.

Labour will always be poor. Yet it can be more professional, and with effort and imagination, it can raise enough for the push to power. Once there, it must immediately introduce state funding of political parties, not throw the opportunity away as it did last time. There would also be justice in doing the same to Tory funds as they attempted to do to ours, by requiring shareholder ballots for all company political donations with full publication of both donations and company accounts. He who can combine sweet revenge with natural justice is a happy politician. But that must await office.

Some business people are sympathetic to Labour. Many recognize that they would do better under a Labour government. All have an interest in seeing politics healthy, opposition effective, government kept on its toes. So Labour should appeal to firms, starting with the biggest, emphasizing the benefits of Labour's proposals for the economy and the failures of the Tories, pointing out that keeping a government in check and making it justify its policies requires a vigorous, independent opposition. The party should offer companies opportunities to meet and consult with the shadow spokespeople to exchange views and discuss policy. The response could be substantial, at least from enlightened firms and managers. It would certainly provide a way of finding out just how many of them there are.

Labour's present reality is the dictatorship of the activist because a mass party of the old type cannot work in an age of mass leisure. Politics is, for most people, a peripheral and intermittent interest. So we need a political mail order party, with postal contact, a point of input. An effective party needs a much bigger base of inactive members so that the activists can work and act in their name but subject to their ultimate control and qualified by knowledge of their views and wishes. With a genuine mass membership, exercising control by democratic votes in postal ballots rather than pathetic attendance at boring and unnecessary meetings, the party can rebuild and ease away from the unions.

The Labour Party needs the unions; the unions need the Labour Party. Every social democratic party is integrated with them but in none do they dominate as they do here. The rest of the membership is so atrophied that the unions not only control the party but, even worse, are seen to do so. The results are mostly benign: money, sense, roots, a restraint on the follies of party members, a shrewd realism, for the unions are essential to Labour and mainly work for its good. Yet anomalies such as the block vote (with the party looking like the TUC's poodle) cannot be justified, even on the grounds that our own members are not fit to be trusted. It is time now to change the 1918 settlement and shift the balance of the relationship to make the party more independent, with its own free-standing structure formulating its own policies and dealing with the unions as independent organisations via leadership consultation Keep the affiliation fee but only allow unions a slice of the vote at conference that is equal to the numbers they can persuade to pay £1.00 for individual associate members. Maintain close relations with the unions through the Joint Council of Labour on a consultative basis but look to the whole TUC, as well as the affiliated unions and attempt to permeate union leaderships with Labour people. The affiliates should nominate one-third of the reconstituted National Executive, with another third from the PLP and elected by it and another third selected by postal ballot by all members. This should be the managing body of the party.

Labour is a programmatic party, policy at its core. It claims to involve its members in its formulation yet its structures are a series of baffles to prevent that power being used in the way that the members want, while leadership is carried out by subterfuge. So unions and constituencies that do not want to dominate, but instead would rather be heeded, are forced to amplify and even to try and impose their views because they are not listened to. Rows replace rational discussion, frustration drives out satisfaction, fudges and formulae result rather than clarity and conviction. The alternative is more leadership from the sales force – the Parliamentary Party – with the rank and file contributing suggestions, discussing and propagating.

Policy cannot spring from bright ideas and dogmatic assertions, particularly after they have been rendered incomprehensible by 'compositing' and then exposed to a debate more like a rummage through a rubbish bin than any logical analysis. It is a process, not a battleground, and rationality is neither left nor right. Policy should be formulated from the top, researched by the research department and discussed through the party structure, starting with constituencies and then at regional conferences, with the whole business conducted as an educative and propaganda exercise.

The annual conference cannot decide policy, and should not try. Suggestions should flow from the membership into the regional conferences, which would discuss them and, if appropriate, refer them, together with the more detailed proposals of the PLP, to a continuous policy-making body. Springing out of the present policy review committees, this would be a Policy Council with, like the NEC, a tripartite composition but all members voting as individuals with neither block votes nor mandates. Working up from green paper discussion to generate wide interest and involvement, such a structure would allow suggestions to be ventilated without the automatic assumption that they are party policy as soon as spoken, as happens now to conference resolutions. Such an approach would involve the members in the way they want: being heard and having a say, rather than trying to achieve a mythical power and then having to be frustrated.

The new leadership election system is a doomsday machine that cannot be invoked lightly lest it blow up the party. It involves the unions in decisions for which they are neither organized nor qualified to take. It makes those sections of the party which know least about the candidates dominant in their choosing. It discounts the parliamentary judgement which should be the pre-eminent consideration. It is far too cumbersome, entrenching leaders in a way that no party can afford. It makes popularity in the party and conformity to its prejudices and mythologies major influences, when the party should be looking for stature, general popularity and ability.

Yet having opted to select leaders by a system which, in the *tabula rasa* of opposition, could only throw up Neil Kinnock or someone very like him, Labour will then grumble as the chosen ones rise above the origins that created them, the better to lead Labour to the wider world. It will grumble the more because they cannot be changed, even if the party wants them to be. Our leaders are there until they choose to go, a decision which is theirs, not the party's. Their part of the bargain is to get on with the job.

Neil Kinnock has concentrated on making Labour electable and is, therefore, the right leader – not only the best leader we have got, as R. A. Butler might put it, but better than we deserve. His achievement has been enormous by the standards of 1979–83, substantial by those of the Wilson era, and a saner party would understand that the task of cleaning its own Augean stables has kept him from establishing the commanding public presence he needs. That can only come as the pendulum swings back to Labour, producing the media glow which arrives only with a 15 per cent poll lead and the respect that the deferential media feel for someone with prospects. As a leader more clear headed than Callaghan, and more principled than Wilson, Neil Kinnock lacks only stature. That comes with time. The way to be a leader is to lead.

His other qualifications are substantial. He has a humanity, a realism and a lust for power. He brings from his working-class background the genuine passion given to few in a party of lecturers and journalists *manqués*. His approach and his reforms, which are pulling Labour back to the middle of the road, have been right. He inspires the party. He has warmth, passion and slowly re-emerging charm and humour, which he communicates well to a television electorate. To lead Labour to the right, the leader must come from the left to exploit the friendships, contacts and trust he or she has there. The choice of Neil Kinnock was correct, but it makes his job that of reform or bust.

The next leader will be chosen for different reasons and purposes, a decision that would be helped by a return to PLP election. This time, the leaders would be on a short-term contract, subject to performance, reviewable and renewable every two years, rather than facing distracting challenges that disturb the party and cost a fortune. Today, leaders seem to burn out and fade more quickly than an Attlee or a Churchill, so they must be disposable. We ask too much of our leaders: to be figurehead, committee chair, inspirer of the faithful, philosopher of socialism, quiz kid with all the answers, TV personality, parliamentary gladiator, charisma-idol, and leader of a party incapable of being led.

Not even Super-Woman could do it all, and in any case, a coalition party really needs leadership of the Attlee type, strengthened by a stronger collective backing from a Shadow Cabinet, which should play a much greater part than it has. If the leader appoints good people to the right jobs and lets them get on with it, he can concentrate on the party's public face and on parliamentary battle. Though overflowing with talent, Labour's present Shadow Cabinet has taken far too much of a back seat, distancing itself from Neil Kinnock, not even asserting its influence in matters of obvious folly. It should be an effective part of the collective leadership of the party, its best and brightest working as a team, not a set of careerists accidentally thrown together and all pursuing their own fortunes at the expense of the others or even of the leader, seeing their hope in his failure. By enhancing its collective authority, it can become a powerful counter to the one-person band on the other side, and project Labour in the only way a coalition can be saleable – as a team.

Labour's structural weaknesses should have been tackled before its policy, for any policy that emerges through the present structures is premature ejaculation. The policy review process is better than the chaos that went on before, but it is still too rushed and has elements of the old bamboozlement technique: short-circuiting conference by presenting it with a *fait accompli*, inviting it to swallow a pre-cooked meal and assuming it has then accepted what it did not really want in the first place. Good policy would spring more naturally from a healthy party.

Labour is now ready to be led rather than pandered to. During this a rare window of opportunity the blocks are fragmented, members bemused, the party ready to accept leadership if it is told what it must do and why. Those socialist parties that have been successful in the 1980s – the French Socialists, the Australasian parties, the Swedish SAP – all changed substantially in the 1970s, laying the groundwork for their present success. Labour has to do the same but from a position of weakness, for the others were and are genuinely national parties while Labour is tied to the past, the North, the trade unions, the traditional working class. If it remains locked in its ghetto rather than reaching out to the new, it will fade away. Labour must be bigger than the sum of its components, and as broad as the nation, reaching out to everyone and everywhere. Margaret Thatcher has set the example by transforming the Tory Party, throwing overboard Heath and all his works, and appealing to a new anti-tax, anti-state, anti-union, pro-incentive, pro-market yobboism. On that tide, she rode to power as the avenging angel of middle-class prejudice. Labour does not have to stand existing policies on their heads. But it must change to catch the wave, or even be lifted by a ripple.

Had we but world enough, and time, this coyness, Labour, were no crime. We haven't. The present, piecemeal reform proposals are the bare minimum, and marching backwards to change does not create a united, enthusiastic party. Everyone feels bamboozled, if only because they are. The tide of change that took the SPD to Bad Godesberg and upwards stopped in Britain in 1960. Take advantage of it now, belatedly but wholeheartedly, or harden in the postures of decline, becoming irrelevant, warmhearted, right. A cuddly party full of decent values and people. Left behind by history.

Because Labour is a life experience rather than a party, its politicians can't think beyond these bounds. Yet the view that 'there is nothing to do other than what we have done in the past only better' is a formula for failure. We are talking about a revolution: the real revolution of consumer democracy, bringing together all who lose from the tyranny of the Tory minority into a new majority in broad coalition. We can only do it if we identify with them and their common interests, exposing the lies and distortion on which that dictatorship is built, convincing them of the enormous benefits of change, and of Labour's competence to carry it out. At the moment, they are disorganized and Labour is ghetto-ized. Our priority must be to give them the power to throw out their oppressors and a way, through a people-friendly party, to change what they do not like.

This change in attitudes is the revolution appropriate to a different society. That requires a different party but one that Labour can become if it is clear about what it is doing. Socialism is still saleable in consumer politics, its objectives still as relevant, but it must be promoted and put over by new methods if Labour is to be saved and Britain rebuilt.

7
Beyond Socialism

Socialism is Labour's joy and its curse. The joy is a noble, unselfish aspiration, a vision of a better world, a goal to work for, elevating the compromises and manoeuvrings of politics to a higher purpose. It is also a curse because every kind of lunatic can shelter under its broad banner, its name is used to justify any folly, and it has become as irrelevant to the wider public as theosophy, though with the sinister overtones that the latter would have acquired had Karl Marx been Annie Besant's lover. Socialism is our leper's badge. As such, it is the essence of our problem. An aspiration that the community does not share and we cannot define, cutting us off, turning us inwards, talking, in our own language, to ourselves. As if St Patrick had arrived in Ireland speaking 2nd-century Aramaic and clutching the *Guide Michelin* for the Holy Land.

Exercise or exorcise? Should socialism be left living, uneasily and possibly unwell, within the Labour Party? Or should it be consigned to a late grave in a world where Marx is dead, Crosland dead and Tony Benn isn't feeling any too good? Labour is obliged to pretend that socialism lives. It is the language in which everything – from pure hypocrisy to aspirations more noble than any that could be dreamed of in Thatcher's philosophy – must be phrased to be acceptable. It is Labour's breastplate and back protector, for everything must be defended as 'socialist' to escape attack in a party whose members are perpetually posing as more socialist than thou.

The result is confusion. Is socialism an end or a means? State or process? Aspiration or status quo? No one poses the questions for fear of being thought unsocialist, and a generation of rising Labour hopefuls feel obliged to advance careers by writing books defining, developing, expounding or expanding socialism. They waste their time because they are talking to the party not the world, ending up with results that no one outside reads because they are not interested and no one inside reads either because they know it all. These are the hallmarks of a sect. As with all sects, the adherents like it that way, taking comfort from their own paranoia because socialism makes them feel different. If there were too many socialists, they would be far less happy. If socialism were to become popular, they would dislike it intensely.

Attitudes towards socialism have become ever more schizophrenic as the realization dawns that it is incomprehensible and counter-productive outside the contracting bounds of the Pale, whether pink or red. Roy Jenkins has not given it a thought in years. David Owen had to go through the second edition of *Face the Future* (the first of his many, different prescriptions for the regeneration of Britain, and the only one to have survived into a further edition) to cut every mention of it. Mrs Thatcher has dedicated herself to eliminating it everywhere, from Britain to Poland, under the assumption that it is the same in both countries. If she is not stopped, she will do so, although it will have taken her slightly longer than her destruction of the unions, full employment, the economy, the welfare state and democracy.

Even within the Labour Party there is the same confusion. What is socialism? Tony Benn has spent his life, at least since 1970, defending it, publishing arguments for it, standing for the leadership to proclaim it, but never saying what it is. The Left sees it as something the party has abandoned, the Right see it as something so bland that it is a truism, and the public, their blood curdled by the press, see it as something awful. Labour requires everything to be justified in the name of socialism, not as a vote (and power) getter, and if it cannot be so justified, Labour will, out of hand, reject it, no matter how relevant, how popular, how electorally advantageous. Socialism has become a charm worn to ward off middle-class spirits. We split over it, argue about it, defend it, betray it, but we never actually define it in any way that both public and party can now accept.

Life is difficult for a party with a creed that no one can define. Many do not want to. It's nicer, or nastier, that way. Opponents can conjure any available bogeyman from Soviet

Communism to Paddy Ashdown: Supporters can designate anything of which they approve. Herbert Morrison's 'Socialism is what Labour governments do' becomes, for activists, what they do not do. Everyone brings to socialism their own interpretation, malign or benign. The dictionary definition – 'Public ownership of the means of production, distribution and exchange' – seems less relevant when, back in the USSR, Gorbachev is resiling on the faith, and in Australia, New Zealand and Spain, socialist governments are deregulating busily and selling state enterprises to balance budgets. Even here, its most enthusiastic advocates now have no higher aim than to halt the shrinking of the public sector though the process is invisible as Labour commits itself to renationalizing everything that the government sells and then, one by one, forgets. Renationalizing just to vary the mix of a mixed economy would be perverse, but it has become a badge of socialist virility for some.

All this demonstrates the need for a new definition of socialism and what it is about. That problem is older than the party. Socialism is an ethos of its time that must be continuously updated to suit new circumstances. The doctrine sprang from the needs of the mass working class in the emerging industrial society. Defenceless because unorganized against the dominance of capitalism and the power of ownership, the workers looked to the state as their ally, and the agent of their advance. The state was the collective will of the people and it alone could provide the leverage to control the irresponsible power and excesses of private capitalism, ownership and wealth. It could regulate wages and conditions, further equality by redistributive taxation and build the better society. Controlling capitalism meant public ownership, the only form that collective control could take at that time, for in the world before the managerial revolution, ownership was power. That had to be vested in the people by structures designed to extend democratic control over the economy by putting it under governments elected by popular majorities. From this sprang that triumph of socialism: the Morrisonian Corporation. London Transport turned into a system of economics.

The history of social democracy is one of the redefinitions of socialism, a process of continuous creation starting with Bernstein's defence of real politics rather than ideology. Bernstein's revisionism emphasized political practicalities as opposed to those who looked to the inevitability of Marx's predictions. In Britain, socialism was always more practical, concentrating on advancing people through trade union-based 'Labourism' rather than socialism. Pragmatism was the approach of a British Labour Party that has become obsessively ideological only in its dotage. Labour's education was in the school of hard knocks, not ivory tower. There was, however, an internal debate and a tension between the practical and the theoretical, those who looked to power and those who were obsessed with a better world, and in 1923 and 1929–31, when Labour governments held office (not power), socialism became the excuse of those who refused to be soiled by the necessary compromises – a form of escapism that then flourished, with every other extremism, in the 1930s.

That escape route was gradually blocked by the pragmatic trade unions who weaned Labour from infantilism and brought it down to earth. Their practical preoccupations encouraged the development of realistic strategies of social and economic reform based on Keynesian economics and welfare spending, rather than on socialist theory. Labour was to work with capitalism to remedy its deficiencies rather than build the socialist state that no one really believed in any more. Socialism shifted from ownership to management, from control to planning and the rational uses of resources to avoid the waste and follies of the 1920s and '30s. Public ownership of the means of production was narrowed to those industries that were failing the nation, such as coal and the railways, to allow the rest to function better.

Such was the essence of British socialism, until the revisionism of the 1950s took that practical emphasis one stage further by arguing that the basic restructuring had all been done by the Labour government of 1945–51. Socialism now meant building on these foundations and using the resulting affluence to make life better for people. Gaitskell was revisionism's leader. C. A. R. Crosland its philosopher. His *Future of Socialism* shifted the whole debate away from ownership and planning to consumerism. Socialism was no longer about means but ends. The prime end was equality. The fundamental problems of capitalism had been solved by Keynes, so socialists could get growth and spread it fairly among the people by using public spending to improve the quality of their lives. This had the incidental benefit of sustaining the demand that an expanding economy required. Its basis was welfare, affluence and growth, which would allow the process of redistribution towards equality to be painless. Socialism was reconciled with the consumer society, Labour with affluence.

Yet revisionism, too, was a creation of its own time – the period of post-war affluence. The emphasis on equality fitted in with the emergence of a mass consumer society: more equality and more growth signalled more demand, more evenly (and effectively) distributed. Demand management through Keynesian economics meant that it was no longer necessary to control the economy, merely to manage it for growth, leaving it to professional managers to run specific firms because, after the managerial revolution, ownership was less important in capitalism. This was consumer socialism: maximum well-being achieved by generating growth, as the agency of the advance of the people.

Crosland's *Future of Socialism* was, therefore, a product of its time, though most of what it says still applies today. In saying that socialism was not about public ownership and the state but equality and the fair society, he laid the basis for the two Labour governments that came after, even if they did not achieve his aims. He also set basic goals that still hold true. The real problem was that the economic growth on which everything was predicated was never achieved. Without it, redistribution became painful and was, therefore, never really attempted. Life never improved enough to satisfy rising expectations. Socialism never delivered on the hopes it aroused. The public spending needed to improve the quality of life had to be financed out of taxes and produced a reaction among those bearing the tax burden. Fairness and altruism never become the dominant forces that Crosland envisaged. Instead, growing dislike, division and envy became the inevitable characteristics of decline. Crosland's socialism is less relevant today only because we have failed to achieve the growth on which it was to be based, not because his theory is outdated.

The Wilson government, with a majority to do anything, did little to achieve the most basic objective of growth. Other priorities – maintaining the parity of sterling, sustaining an over-heavy defence commitment, showing that Labour could be a better defender of orthodoxy than the Tories – were all higher in Harold's list. Labour fulfilled every trivial promise in a long manifesto, a list that was religiously crossed off. The party failed only on the basic undertaking to make the people better off. That failure reveals something deep in Labour's psyche. Wanting to prove itself respectable, it clings to orthodoxy. It does best when defending this, unlike the Tories, who have the self-confidence to take risks. They have always been the party which has gone for rapid growth. Labour defended the exchange rate, though devaluation was implicit in all that it promised and, without, it, it was doomed to continuous deflation with no prospect of growth. It then sought solace in stupidity's last defence: it was 'doing its duty'; this was the medicine of the economy, which would bring it back to health, through responsibility, sense and discipline.

That was the role it resumed in 1974. The Heath government had unleashed a massive dash for growth, a boom-and-bust drive that ended (because it coincided with the Arab oil price rise) in bust. Labour came in to clean up the mess. With the cooperation of the trade unions, it did so, saving the nation through the combination of a tough incomes policy, keeping spending as high as orthodoxy (and the IMF) would permit, and a fair distribution of sacrifices. Britain was brought through its worst economic difficulties since the war, but Labour and socialism were not now the midwives of the new but the Elastoplast of the old.

Because of that failure, socialism faced adjustment to a new, far more difficult society, satiated but dissatisfied, wanting equality but not its disciplines, both bovine and bolshy. Britain may not be characterized by success and satisfaction, but neither is it totally about failure and division. The national

characteristic can be best described as 'disaffluence': a dissatisfied semi-affluence; a disgruntled, selfish, resentful
society, hankering after predictable certainties reacting rather
than knowing. Politics, because they have been a process of
failure, the continuous mobilization of excuses, are of diminishing salience and interest. A disillusioned electorate are privatizing them as they opt out and establish their own territory and
privacy. Affluence, the age of mass demand, has given way to
more segmented demand – financial differences, specialized
markets. The monoliths are breaking down but have not
broken to give way to pluralism. The privatization of lifestyles,
the establishment of separate worlds has spread with home
ownership and its joys, including the leverage of credit. So the
old rallying cries of class solidarity are less relevant; old needs
no longer so strongly felt. The old reflexes still work but in
fewer people. The old signposts point now in confusing directions. Labour has drifted, out of touch, with no ethos, no
central doctrine, no way of striking chords with the privatized
nation.

Labour looks to revolution. The nation is conservative. It
does not respond to calls for drastic change because the
problems of poverty, unemployment and deprivation, glaring
in the past, have been sectionalized and privatized, forced on
minorities, not whole classes. The subclass retires from the
world in shame to close the door on its misery, rather than
taking it into the streets to stir the conscience of the majority.
Revolution comes from felt grievances in an age of improvement, not from the general decline and deprivation that characterized Britain in the 1970s and will again. Decline ex-
acerbates division and Fascism, not altruism and concern. In a
modern society, mass myths are also privatized: inner visions
of desires; self-images rather than social evangels; the revolution in the self, not society; the ego, not the nation. Such a
world is hardly recognizable as the product of the simple
benefits of growth that Crosland advanced in the 1950s, but
only because it has not had the growth. The idea of progress
has not been abolished, but faith in it and its possibilities has
weakened.

Political doctrines – socialism, conservatism, liberalism –
are not bodies of eternal truth floating above the ages like

Platonic images projected on to the wall of the cave of the future. They are modified by the times. The climate has become colder for socialism, and Labour's own failures have chilled it. A party that began by offering working people a better deal, and which certainly delivered it from 1945 to 1951, did all too little for the working class in the 1960s, and found itself straining their loyalties, union ties and class solidarity by cutting their standards of living in the 1970s. That caused socialism to be associated with fairer shares of misery, not the real vision of perpetual betterment sustained by real improvement. Rather than building a better world, Labour and socialism were directing their efforts to keeping a rickety machine going, yet the machine was rickety because they had not had the courage or the ability to rebuild and expand it.

The Left had always regarded the Right as anti-intellectual, Conservatism as the creed of priest and prejudice, the stupid party. In the 1970s, the roles reversed. Economic failure brought forth a crop of 'New Right' thinking. As Buddha foretold, the no-mind no-thinks no-thoughts about no-things, so much of it was non-sense. The chorus of complaint against welfare and the state that would have been totally banished by success had merely been overlain by affluence. It now burst forth with failure, carrying a new intellectual gloss, and was suddenly fashionable but still basically the same: a critique of the state, especially in its 1970s corporate form, as the enemy of freedom; a case for markets as an alternative to management, which had failed; a fiscal case for incentives and low taxes, a theory that spread like other lunacies from California and was sustained by the hostile reaction to the tax structure that pressed further down the income scale in an age of low growth.

It was all pure nonsense, and nothing better illustrates the extent of its own rigid stultification than the inability of socialism to rebut that collection of trite *non sequiturs* collectively described as Thatcherism. It gained power by blaming the victims of Britain's economic failure, the workers and the poor (a.k.a. 'scroungers') and set out to make their position worse rather than tackle the real causes. Insofar as it rejected the state for the market, intervention for individualism and the communal for the ego, it was simple nonsense – of a type that it did not dare apply to moral matters when nanny was put in power. Government is a question of holding balances, not enthroning extremes. Insofar as it shifted those balances away from the post-war settlement and in the direction of Gladstonian Liberalism (drained of its moral element), Thatcherism was merely counter-productive because it failed to recognize that both government and the nation-state are a form of intervention in the market. Insofar as it was just a question of cutting public spending and hence taxes, it was merely social revenge – a reverse Robin Hood transfer of power from the bottom to the top of the ladder, excused by a fallacious argument about incentives.

Thatcherism was brought to power by accident and by the failure of every alternative, was held there by the acquiescence of an electorate that had given up hope and by the political deadlock, and was never implemented to the degree that would have discredited it totally. It was, however, used to justify making society more unfair, tax less progressive, and industry – the driving force for equality with its skills, union strength and high pay – weaker. That such rubbish could have gone uncontested and be seen as definitively shifting the balance of debate to the right is a mark not of its own intellectual strength, but of the extent to which socialist thought and the Left had atrophied and degenerated into slogans and cant. When the Left's answer to Thatcherism was 'Maggie! Maggie! Maggie! Out! Out! Out!' it was certain evidence that Labour had become the stupid party, not that the Conservatives were the more intelligent.

The nonsense was allowed to look exciting and new because petrified socialism failed to defend its own propositions, regarding the New Right as so incredible that no one in their Left mind could believe it. The trouble was, the electorate no longer was, and socialism was part of a status quo with which they were unhappy. Defending precluded change. Just to think about whether there was value in the jerry-built structure of clumsy nationalized industries and a mean bureaucratic welfare state was considered treasonable. Socialism was not being rethought, developed and updated, because its adherents had retreated into different foxholes, all of them too busy defending their own assumptions and positions by throwing bricks at other 'socialists'. Argument drove out thought, and Labour ceased to think. Socialism almost died in the Callaghan era. Labour was taken by surprise by New Right ideas that it had not considered worth refuting, and was flabbergasted when folly swept past it to power, and, more amazingly, to popularity. It blamed the nation: people had become selfish. Dismay turned into disorientation when the reaction washed away the gains that Labour had thought indestructible and built a nasty new world of its own. None of this was dreamed of in socialism's ideology. The party's physical breakdown was paralleled by socialism's nervous breakdown, a shellshock similar to that of recruits sent 'over the top' in the First World War.

Progress had not only stopped but had gone into reverse. A belief in the inevitability of progress, of socialism borne forward on the tide of history, was fundamental to the creed. Jerusalem would still be built. Yet Margaret Thatcher was digging up the foundations and reducing to ruins the pathetic edifice so far run up, to build a Wimpy version of Sodom if not Gomorrah. The electorate hardly shared Labour's concerns. Ten years down a dead-end street, the nation still shows no desire to rush back to Jerusalem for Labour had abandoned education and persuasion. It had ceased to explain what it was doing, and the 'City on the hill' was seen by the people, not as a noble aspiration that Labour still could achieve, but as a symbol of bureaucracy, corporatism, taxation, deflation, incomes policy, vain, unvindicated assurances, devious politics and bitter rows. Small wonder so few came into the streets to protest Thatcherism.

Labour compounded the nightmare into which it had drifted. Socialism had become a necessary hypocrisy, not a living, breathing, changing creed; everything had to be 'socialist' or Left (hard or detumescent) to be accepted; not lived up to but conformed to, a protective cover. There was no point in defining it because even discussing it stirred fundamental disagreements that were better not aired. So Labour coasted along, constitutionally committed to the public ownership of the means of production, distribution and exchange which it did not actually believe in, preferring not to open the Pandora's box that was, by definition, socialism surviving by covering itself in a rigid carapace.

That stance sanctioned claims that any rubbish was socialism, and in the bitter, more divided and hence more ideological age of the 1970s, 57 varieties duly emerged. The thoughtless are never wordless. In those strange times, the politics of unthink drove out those of reason on the Labour side, just as they had on the Tory. Labour had its nervous breakdown just as the Tories entered the insane phase of their economic policy. With a media like Britain's our madness distracted all attention from theirs.

Leninism justified the vanguard party and its authoritarian attitudes. Trotskyism justified destabilization and insanity. Marxism justified nationalization of 200, 50 (O.N.O.) firms. Syndicalism justified the NUM, and Popularism Liverpool, Lambeth and a host of less successful Town Hall Lansburys all clamouring for a martydom that was readily provided. These constituted socialism's provisional wing. The official wing, too, was split: those who were pro and anti market, those pro and anti growth – none of them inspired with Crosland's daring radicalism or his sense of vision, and none of them prepared to think anew as he had. Socialism had become shades of grey orthodoxy. Left and Right had two things in common: a willingness to prescribe, and a belief that they knew best. Both attitudes were shared by Mrs Thatcher but her platitudes were populist and theirs were not, and unpopular stances coupled with *de haut en bas* attitudes are alien to a pluralistic society that wants to choose for itself not be lectured to. Socialism had even ceased to talk the language of the less-class society. It had become a sulk. General sourness and alienation from the real world were viewed as high principle.

Labour's debate had been reduced to trading badge slogans, though at least badges get read. As John Stuart Mill had seen, the fatal tendency of humanity to stop thinking about a thing when it is no longer doubtful was the cause of half human errors. Having stopped thinking, Labour failed to take the New Right's attack on its world seriously. European socialist parties, particularly in Scandinavia, devote massive efforts to party education, developing common bonds of thought and conditioning, trained reflexes as well as new ideas and new ways of advancing socialism. Labour got tired of teaching in the 1940s and of thinking after 1963. It lived off its accumulated capital for a decade thereafter, never investing, never renewing, never thinking, never educating simply surviving by high-wire antics under Harold Wilson, by dull, dogged duty under Jim Callaghan.

This failure occurred because the roots of socialism had atrophied. For some, it was a corpse preserved in ice. For most, it had ceased to be relevant, an intellectual exercise, not the product of a felt experience. Labour was (as it was bound to be) a bourgeois party but different from other such parties in that it continued to pretend to be both socialist and proletarian when it was neither. Socialism was in danger of becoming 'disorganized hypocrisy'.

After the war, Labour had faced a conscious choice: administer the bourgeois state better, or go down the socialist road. Motivated by duty it had not chosen socialism, which was, in fact, a class road. That would have been a massive new beginning involving rebuilding society, not as a middle-class, individualistic enterprise, but on the basis of community to be managed by the class institutions of solidarity, unions, and communal support – a stronger and fairer welfare state, managed for fairness, the people in power not their bourgeois bosses. This may have been what the mass of British people wanted in 1945, but it required a more effective discipline than obtained in British unions, a clearer vision than found in British Labour and economic growth far greater than Britain ever generated to make the community accept that discipline was paying off. Such a course was left to the cold Swedes. Labour chose mish-mash, sentiment and rhetoric.

The party – its leadership middle class and uneasy with the working-class ethic – never saw the choice. Rather than setting out to build a new world by standing society on its head, the Labour leadership's aim was to earn the approbation of the City, finance, the Establishment, the editorials, by showing that they could manage the system and deliver the support of the workers. They really wanted to transform, the working class into people like them – i.e. middle class, Oxbridge, conformists – and to create a world fit for grammar school kids, that most alienated section of the proletariat, to live in. In building the grammar school society they killed the distinctive ethics of working-class solidarity, from which they had escaped, and eliminated its sense of community, fairness, duty and togetherness, by destroying working-class life and abusing its ethics and disciplines for their own purposes, usually temporary ones centred on the survival of Labour governments. The only counter-pole to the glittering society of 'Admass' – a working-class world romanticized, as it died, by Richard Hoggart, Brian Jackson and Jeremy Seabrook – was destroyed by Labour governments, councils, planners, social workers and all the other do-gooders and bleeding-hearts who spilled the blood of a working class they did not understand because they, at least, had been rescued from it. Socialism was destroyed as a living instinct by the world from whence it sprang being pulled down and nothing put in its place. The workers got little return on their investment in Labour governments, the unions on their incomes policy, the movement on its solidarity, the aristocracy of Labour on their skills. Labour never delivered the growth and well-being that could have satisfied them. Yet it provided no alternative either because it had run out of ideas, inspiration, socialism.

Bevan thought that the working class had thrown away an historic opportunity that would never recur. The party had rushed down the path of consumer socialism only to end up with a shoddy consumer society sustained by an inadequate economy – the middle class, writ shabbier. Harold Wilson portrayed that process as 'white-heated purpose'. In fact, the economy was not even being managed for growth but was drifting with the tide of consumerism. Trade union solidarity was wasted in crisis management to cut working-class wages, not improve them. Wants were endlessly stimulated, not satisfied. Britain was not being built by discipline and investment, but bought off by consumer affluence. The unions never developed the institutional strength, the centralized collective power, the will or the disciplines to deliver the necessary *quid pro quo*s that genuine participation in the management of a solidarity society would have required. They were coolies, not partners. They reacted accordingly, with clumsy help and intermittent peasant revolts.

Today, it is too late. The old bases of solidarity are gone. The institutions of union discipline are not now up to the job, the members sullen. The combination of Keynesian economic management and incomes policy had been so badly abused in decline that Labour dare not envisage it for growth. Incomes policy will be necessary, but since 1978, Labour has hardly talked about it within the party, and has never dared to negotiate with the unions for an incomes policy deal in return for changes in Tory union law – the only logical approach to organizations since they are, by definition, about negotiation. Neither failure stops Labour from being tainted with the image of cutting take-home pay because its reaction to Tory booms is puritanical distaste. Here is no bright vision, no new dawn. Just a semi-socialist mess that no one has much faith or belief in any more. Labour had come to be a party without a soul, socialism a creed without substance. The rhetoric was still there but little of the substance, and they had no idea how to get it.

Realization that the noblest aspiration had become an empty shell, coupled with shock at the hegemony of Thatcherism, triggered the first nervous breakdown ever experienced by a political party. Labour moved into four years of psychiatric treatment by other lunatics. It did not recover so much as come through. Neil Kinnock, a tough-minded realist, had the intelligence and integrity to shed the child's clothes he had worn to rise, but not the intellectual charisma to make his new realism glitter as brightly as his invocations of the old ethics. He had a clear, simple vision of a society based on values, but the party itself was a socialist vacuum.

The new revisionists tried to reassure the party with a massive diet of prescription, mostly telling Labour what it should do or what groups it should appeal to (usually black or female) or what issues (usually environmental) it should hit without saying how, and socialists where they should go without saying how to get there. Philosophically, the new revisionists chose the least-brutal approach, telling the party that it was still, of course, socialist, just as they were (and had to be), but socialism was something different to what the party rank and file, and everyone else, had thought it to be. 'Socialism without the state' would be an excellent description had Evan Luard not already used it for the title of his wishy-washy prescription for community politics just before he deserted to the SDP to fail to practise it. Others followed down the same path, all concerned to transmute socialism into something more cuddly and acceptable. Michael Meacher, furthest to the left, gave it a human face (with steel-rimmed glasses) by defining socialism as a process, something that was always going on, where the forces of the market and the tyrannies of money and power had to be continuously humanized, organized and planned for the benefit of the majority, the assumption here being that Labour would be in power to do that. Bryan Gould was bolder, building on the work of the Fabian Socialist Philosophy Group to define socialism – in an interpretation later enlarged (and better popularized) by Roy Hattersley – as 'Freedom'. Like Kravchenko, both choose freedom as a political philosophy, pointing out that, rather than levelling for the sake of equality, imposing the disciplines of the corporate state or repressing diversity by knocking the heads of the tallest poppies, what socialists really wanted to do was set lots more poppies free to grow. Only socialism could provide the mass of people with the platform, which had allowed those with wealth and education to advance and benefit the élite.

The equal society was free. To any previous generation of socialists, such a truism would have been breathtakingly obvious. Yet it still ignored all the theoretical problems: How far should equality be taken? How far could Labour curtail the freedom of wealth, power, business and capital? It also said nothing about how to get there because, in the effort to please, the new prescription eschewed discipline, solidarity, unions, the authoritarian antics of some Labour authorities and incomes policy. Here was an escape from the real world, not a philosophy. It made as little mention of fraternity as it did of equality. It demonstrated the weakness of markets but failed to say how to manage them. It tried to appeal directly to the new 'free to choose' consumer society, but if freedom was the end, growth had to be the key, and no one quite knew how to turn it. Indeed, the logical conclusion should have been that since the free market methods of Mrs Thatcher and the 'Rogernomics' of the New Zealand Labour government worked, they must surely be legitimate. If socialism means ends not means, and the end is growth and freedom, then anything that produces one or the other is socialism. Fortunately for the theory, neither Roger nor Margaret were particularly successful, as any Keynesian could have predicted. Yet just defining socialism as freedom did not explain why. So the only real benefit from the new philosophy was that Labour could move towards a British version of the US Democratic Party, with the same vague commitment of universal goodwill, though not perhaps the same myths, bonds or cleverness, and still pass as socialist.

When Hattersleyism was condensed into the new statement of party principles adopted by the 1988 conference, that document did not even mention fairness. The omission was glaring because fairness has always been a basic aspiration of the working class, and one of the strongest feelings of the British people. They do not know what is right or wrong, they define 'fairness' selectively and are never sure exactly what it means, yet they still have a strong feeling for what is fair, not fair, and a fair go. The concept is philosophically unsatisfactory because ill defined: one person's fairness could be another's ruin. Yet except for the prickly middle class and the eccentrics it nurtures, the British have never cared much about freedom, outside of the Last Night of the Proms, but they do have a gut instinct for fairness even if they can usually only express it by reacting against something thought of as unfair. In 1988, no one was defining it, least of all a sectional Labour Party, many of whose instincts did not seem to be at all fair.

Those unwilling to put all their egos in one basket looked to the old French Revolutionary trio of Liberty, Equality and Fraternity. Each of these three gods in our pantheon has been mobilized as *primus inter* socialist *pares*: Equality by Crosland, Liberty by Hattersley and Gould, Fraternity by David Lipsey. Yet equality also poses problems. As with fairness, most people have a feeling for equality, particularly if it advances them, but they do not want to be the equal of too many others, especially in a consumer society encouraged to express its individualism via small differentations and nuances. In the 'go for it' age, people want to be 'someone' rather than equal.

Liberty, meanwhile, is a truism that Mrs Thatcher as its most vocal advocate is likely to discredit. As for fraternity, its meaning, like love's, has been forgotten, particularly in a Labour Party that shows very little for each other.

More usefully, Bernard Crick has combined liberty, equality and fraternity by arguing that socialism is the end product of inter-breeding between all three elements, one and indivisible, in Labour's blessed trinity. Thus socialism becomes not a state but a process, balancing and adjusting to avoid the errors and excesses of any single element. That requires someone to make the judgement. Sadly, turning a creed into a Pick 'n' Pay mix suggests a jesuitical balancing act, not an easy advertising slogan. We are trying to sell a process, not a message. The same criterion applies to those who have set out to define the real socialism along similar lines to John Rawles by requiring inequalities to justify themselves: philosophy seminars as systems of government, concepts as slogans. Others have sought to integrate markets into socialism while disagreeing on how much and how far.

Each of these were theoretical approaches that would have made socialism a matter of calculus and computers. It was presented as new thinking, but none of it was, for all the elements had been there from the start. External critics of socialism had attacked a straw man by portraying socialism as the state when, in fact, Labour had always looked to the mixed economy, had always accepted markets, had always emphasized the need for judgement, and simply thought that socialists should exercise it in power. Nor did any of the new approaches provide a simple saleable definition. Implicit in all of it was the assumption that Labour and/or its leaders would take on their fragile shoulders the responsibility of making the required judgements on behalf of the great majority, a top downwards approach common to each new definition. Those in the know would decide for a majority not given the same insight and not quite trusted after Tony Benn had discredited activist democracy.

The problem of socialism is like that of the party. It is a distraction. It is counter-productive. Every folly has been justified in the name of socialism, from a discrediting battle for leadership supposedly to defend socialism against betrayal, to the refusal to accept the obvious or compromise with either reality or the electorate. Socialism turns Labour inward. Everything has to be justified in the name of an undefined cloud of gas. Such a situation would be weakening and discrediting enough if there were a sacred text against which doctrine could be checked. Without that, chaos prevails. The Left has always justified its excesses by its self-assumed role as the keeper of the sacred flame, and it boils 100 pans on it. It once had the pure doctrine and still regards itself as the party's self-appointed conscience, but that conscience has become a loud hysteria, not a still, small voice.

According to the Left, strategies have to be socialistically based rather than popular. Yet in consumer politics, they need only be relevant and saleable. Labour's instinctive response of retiring hurt from the world to rethink socialism is therefore counter-productive in politics when the real need is to adjust to change, not reformulate fundamentals. The first step towards modernization after the 1959 electoral defeat was not to change policy or structures but to embark on a highly charged debate about public ownership and whether it should be dropped. After 1979, the party hauled various deep-frozen bits of ideology out of the fridge and threw them at each other. Reform after 1987 began with a new statement of aims and objectives and a policy review that absorbed the thoughts and energies of the party's best brains among a lot of others, while everything else was put into suspended animation. Meanwhile, the real practical problems affecting the people multiplied, and Labour said all too little about the rapid escalation of house prices, the crippling burdens of debt, the inability of the young and poor to break into a housing market, the choking of the transport system, the shoddy decline of roads, sewers, and the public sector, the mounting delays at airports, the emergence of a new class of almost hereditary poor. The real world is difficult for socialists. They feel naked without a theory, perhaps doubly so in a world where theory itself is out of fashion. Yet few wanted an over-aching vision of society in the 1980s. Some were looking to their own internal visions, and most had just given up on ideas and arguments, none of which had ever delivered the goods.

A socialist Labour party must perform a straddle: constantly interpreting its approach in the light of an indefinable doctrine and so unable to listen to the people and decide what it must do in the light of what they want and expect. So the question Labour must face is not whether it can redefine socialism but whether socialism is worth redefining? Does a party any longer need one central ethos in a society where 1000 creeds and 1 million egos flourish and the job of parties is to dilute specifics and appeal to a broad consensus among the electors? That task can be achieved by looking to broad common denominators rather than philosophies or creeds. So is a vision of a new society any longer necessary, or are we just offering to improve the status quo? The answer is that an idealistic party cannot have a vacuum at the core. Yet to fill it, it must study the new society and adjust its values to that.

That society is both confused and confusing. The monoliths have failed: unions and parties to deliver, the state to sustain affluence and growth. People look less to them, tasting power not through the vote but as consumers and home owners. There they are making choices and decisions and have the leverage (as well as the pains and penalties) of credit, often through the power of home ownership. They choose, too, in other aspects of life, even at work, and television dazzles them with a universe of choices, however illusory most of them may be. They advance their lot less through the collective more through themselves.

In Conservative mythology, all these are changes calculated to turn people into Conservatives, but there is no reason why they should. Sociologists have pointed out that the affluence of the 1950s did not result in a fundamental transformation of attitudes: 'a washing machine is a washing machine is a washing machine' not a major change in the psyche of its owner. So today a mortgage equals a burden, equals a drag, equals resentment against the government which puts interest rates up. Yet it is also power, more of it than they feel they have over a state that has become a remote, uncontrollable, incomprehensible force shaping their ends adversely, rough hew them how they may. Against that, their power is limited to the expression of a spluttering resentment, whims through the polls, and meaningless votes, most of which are wasted, every four years. Against shops, banks, even employers, they have more power – still not enough but at least some, including the final power of real choice.

The new society is more cut off from the collective, be it of work and union or class, withdrawing into the home where everything is privatized. Television plugs them into the world, or solaces withdrawal. The family provides satisfactions and insulation. Lifestyle differentiates, inner visions isolate. They are no longer as reachable, as manipulable, as touchable; less persuadable yet more connable because more apathetic and less politically motivated. Politics were more important when major goals remained to be achieved, but in a more satisfied, better entertained world, it has become a background noise. Purists will grumble, but realists should see this as the culmination of what socialists have worked for though achieved at lower levels of education and well-being. The party jerry-built them a world to live in and can hardly complain if they are getting on with it.

A socialism that changes its preoccupations in public relations terms, as the new revisionists have done, from equality to freedom has gone some of the way towards meeting the new consumer democracy, but no one is seriously proposing to abolish freedom, except Margaret Thatcher and even she does so in the name of freedom. So what is needed is not a slogan but an ethos that expresses the basic needs of that society but sits more lightly on the party. A creed that comes *de haut en bas* will not be acceptable, but a sentiment that works with the grain of a freer society and advances its common aspirations is an ethos that can yet provide what the market cannot: a bonding, a feeling of community, a soul. Here is the greatest gap in the lives of the majority. Margaret Thatcher's economic jungle cannot satisfy it, merely frighten the failing, but socialism can by its offering of fraternity. People want involvement and community, hence the proliferation of community, neighbourhood, charity and service groups and activities, all growing more rapidly as people become better off. It is also evidenced by the Prime Minister herself. After years of preaching the 'stand on your own feet' view of captialism, she has suddenly become preoccupied with the concerned citizen, the community, the good Samaritan. Such concerns do not come naturally to her but have been urged on her by her pollsters. Here, they tell her, are the issues that people feel strongly about, the chords you must strike. So must socialism. It would have done so earlier if it had been more concerned with people and the real world than with intellectualizing everything.

The challenge is to free socialism from class. With the working-class ethos fading, like the class itself, a new bonding – *Weltanschauung* – is essential for Labour. Not an ideology but an ethos that is relevant to all the people and which is communicated not via the weakening class monoliths or through a party they do not like or unions they now regard as having a limited instrumental role, but directly to everyone by responding to human, not class, needs. Electors are neither organizable nor reachable as parts of something else. They must be talked to directly as consenting adults, treated as open to persuasion, anxious to be heard. The party must strike chords that reverberate within everyone by talking in terms relevant to their life experience to reach something in their own individual psyche. A universal appeal to people, not a sectional doctrine preached to a class.

Socialism is not about the state, equality or better democracy; it is about community. The essence of socialism is the social as distinct from the individual, the altruistic as opposed to the selfish, the common ground and common good as distinct from the particular and separate. A socialist society is one in which people come together to control the market and manage those aspects of their lives best supported and improved in common, not only the economic and social aspects of their lives but the political ones, too, as they manage their own destinies. Socialism means a society managed by, for and with the majority, to provide for their common needs in the most effective way: by working together. This is not an artificial doctrine but the broad instincts of the people, the simple fact recognized by all, except perhaps by the very rich, that we are one of another, bonded together by our common humanity and our social destiny. Socialism, therefore, is no more than a recognition that we are not isolated individuals, fighting against each other and advancing at the expense of others – the world of P. J. O'Rourke's battle to work – but that we progress together or not at all. The unemployment of one diminishes the product of us all. The poverty of one impoverishes us all. The ignorance or alienation of one endangers all.

The ultimate individualism is not found through isolation and selfishness but achieved in and through society. We attain our maximum individual potential together better than by trampling on each other. This builds on the essential strength of the Labour movement, which has never been economic competence or social realism, virtues that the public misguidedly associates with the Tories while they view us as naïve. Labour's real strength is cooperative ability, an instinct for fairness that appeals to the most attractive elements in that dualism that struggles for supremacy in most souls: altruism, concern, the desire to cooperate.

Personkind has a duality within itself, for everyone is a complex balance of motives and impulses rather than a class stereotype. Selfish impulses are countered by pulls towards community, the individualistic by the concerned, the egotistical by the communal. The mood of the times can tip the balance one way – towards fairness and collective effort during war or after during reconstruction – and then, later, towards selfishness because the collective has either failed or petered out. Yet the tension is always there, and a prolonged period during which the weight of it moves one way provides, by reaction, its own nemesis, beginning a tilt towards the other set of values and impulses. This continuous schizophrenia is never resolved because it comes not from the classes versus the masses, but exists within the individual psyche: the desire to be someone – everyone a king (and every feminist, too) – against the equal desire to be part of the group to pull the bonds and togetherness around for warmth.

Socialism's role is talk to one persona in this schizophrenia: Our input point is the instinct for brotherhood. That does not mean letting Tories monopolize the other, the ego. Community is currently starved and socialism can demonstrate what Mrs Thatcher's failure is steadily making clear – that it is only on the basis of common provision of education, health and social services and on the platform of jobs and well-being that the mass of people have any prospect of 'being someone' by developing their individual talents, abilities and genius. So Labour should appeal to the communal and the concerned side because it alone can satisfy both: fulfilling the aspirations of the mass of the people by giving them the wherewithal that wealth, privilege and education give to the few. That way lies a better society for all. Even if the few do not recognize it quite as readily as Labour.

Socialism therefore offers an escape from the 'prisoner's dilemma' in which Thatcherism traps the nation. The Prime Minister's view of freedom is the survival of the fattest, what she pretends to be freedom can never work, for if government declines to manage markets, their benefits are not maximized but hogged by the powerful, while their failures create distrust. This leaves each and every prisoner in the dilemma of wanting to maximize but knowing that they cannot trust the other players: business to maximize its product; management to be competent; wealth to be fair; unions to influence. So only the law of the jungle – trample or be trampled – is offered as a way out. The prisoners are torn. They want to cooperate because they know rationally that this should offer the best prospect, but lack of trust requires them to grab what is going while they can. It is not certain that they can do either and even less certain that either will yield results. So they are palsied, supporting the unsupportable, grumbling and wanting escape but not doing anything about it. On the other hand, a society run for the benefit of all, a market managed for maximization, a framework in which brute forces are accountable to people provide the only efficient alternatives to Thatcherism's world of greed, buffeted by impersonal forces. Those alternatives used to be known as socialism. It could now be more simply and attractively described as fairness.

Socialism means values, not policies, ends rather than means, the universal not the sectional. As such, it is an evangel directly relevant to the 'better' side of the human duality, not just to the working class that has been its instrument since the early stages and up to now. Such a view will be criticized by the secretarians as dilution, betrayal, sell-out or, even worse, as transforming Labour to the broad appeals and the platitudes of American parties and politicians – the bland leading the blind.

There is no need to argue the point. It is all those things, and none of them before time. American politicians talk to all Americans by mobilizing national myths and images to which all can respond. British society is more divided and its politicians do not have to be as vacuous, but their appeal can be as general – exactly the language that Labour needs to talk. Not to one section via its institutions but to the universe via common aspirations and a sense of community. As socialism takes root in every psyche, finds a home in every heart, it becomes relevant to every life instead of being a remote, alien ideology espoused where people wear woad and speak dialect. Britain's social myths – community, fairness, the common ground, Jack's as good as his master – all fit in well with our socialism, just as America's myth of the frontier does with their individualism. Today's difference is that, in a world of narrowed hope and unfulfilled pluralism, fairness must be seen to be efficiently distributed, effectively focused and reachable by people, not just doled out universally by bleeding hearts. It must be achieved by jobs and by correcting the failures of the market to benefit all, not compensated by universal benefits: an efficient, positive fairness, not a universal, dewey-eyed dole-out. Nevertheless, the instinct for the common, the communal, the bonds that bring together rather than the egotistical (and slightly shameful, still) drives that pull apart is the essence that Labour must now distill. A full life for all cannot be based on a grab for some. Such a gospel will provide the effective counter to Thatcherism which Labour and the people are looking for, given the backing of a party of efficiency and competence.

Instead of addressing 'our people', 'the working class', 'this great movement' or even 'comrades', Labour must speak to all people, citizens, Britons, the world we need to win. In the politics of pluralism, we speak to all or no one. Only on the basis of common impulses, widespread feelings, strongly felt universal concerns can the better society be built. It belongs, after all, to the great majority, not to the few. It is a world yet to be builded here in England's obscene and unpleasant land. Yet the British people, with their deep instinct for fairness, have long aspired to it and still long for it. Despite all we have done to confuse them. Despite all the Tories have done to betray and traduce it.

8

Peoples' Party, Peoples' Agenda

Labour is a serious party, far too serious at times, dedicated to policy and to 'Labour's people'. As problems come up, Labour throws policies at them. When electioneering, it speaks to the party, whose enthusiasm is supposed to radiate out to the wider working class. Both approaches are appropriate to the politics of conditioning, less so to an age of media and consumer politics. In the latter, the electorate chooses as political consumers, not like B. F. Skinner's pigeons. Their wants, images, attitudes are both laid down and stimulated by television with its impressions and moods, and the war is one of sales, not class. So people-pleasing drives party politics. Ideally, parties must sell, not expect Pavlovian reflexes. Yet because the evolution is incomplete, they must do both, transmitting on two frequencies, schizophrenia turned into a political process.

In the politics of people-pleasing, party members, unions and the working class – the centres of Labour's universe – must be taken for granted to win new ranges of support. The Tory party knows this well. Its members have no power, and the interests it represents are almost invisible. Its policies are expressed in popular platitudes, an easier task for them because Conservative extremism translates readily into the vacuities that everyone likes: tax cuts; set the people free; roll back the state. No one knows what all this means but they like the slogans, while Labour's extremism is expressed in ideological terms of nationalize this, equalize that, direct the other – a language few speak.

The people's party and the people must learn to speak to each other. With Labour out of adjustment with its potential market, Britain is force-fed a Thatcherite diet it does not particularly want, by a government most people do not like, whose leader is the second most unpopular prime minister since the war, using methods that are not popular. Opposition is impotent, yet its policies and values are what the public tells the pollsters it wants. The public ideology is not on the political agenda.

People are altruistic. They feel threatened by the changes that Mrs Thatcher has unleashed, worried by national decline, public squalor, increasing social gaps and the disintegration of road and rail. They dislike the ethics of Thatcherism, and many of its consequences. If they voted for policies, they would elect most of Labour's. But not – yet – Labour. Mrs Thatcher has managed to conceal all this disaffection by privatizing politics. She will not change, so politics are irrelevant, argument a waste of time. She is the dignified and the active part of the constitution. All the rest is a distant nuisance and a discrediting preoccupation for odd, quirky people who like rowing with each other, something decent people have as little need of as sex and violence on television. Respectability lies in accepting a cut-price-Catherine-the-Great agenda as normal and rational, anything else as perverse, particularly if it can be slurred by association with the Labour Party. The public has been made to feel guilty about what they really want. In organized form, in the Labour Party, those desires are even subversive. Truth is lies, altruism is subversive, selfishness is service and confusion the norm.

Labour helped this process by abandoning the centre ground and giving up politics for ideology. Most people would not recognize an ideology if it drove over them in a tank, but they know what they do not like. Instead of a coherent political philosophy, something not given even to the Prime Minister, ordinary mortals have a confused mass of assumptions, perceptions, principles – some extreme, some insane, most vague and half understood, altogether classifiable as the 'centre ground' if only because people instinctively avoid extremes. One thing cancels out another. The middle ground is marshy.

People vote for parties for a range of reasons: conditioning, negative dislike of one thing, defending the bad against the far worse, image, associations, even, in rare cases, positive enthusiasm. However, the basic motive is economic. They seek the party that will do best for them. The party must be competent to that end, the people comfortable with it. Association with policies, attitudes and behaviour they dislike makes them uneasy. What they want is some coincidence of values and interests with theirs. If that fails, if the party favours other groups or installs other gods in its shrine, it alienates.

Labour's policy processes are about ideology, not people, and as a programmatic party, it has no means of taking public opinion into account in its decision-making, and little of translating policies into the language of the people who must buy them. It devotes time and effort to splitting on its policy papers and papering over these splits, but little to sales or to adding colouring and flavouring. Yet in a consumer democracy, parties are sales organizations competing for the preferences of an electorate that evaluates them like products. So Labour's approach is bound to fail. The proper combination is policies relevant to the needs of the country, which are also saleable and attractive to those who will benefit from them.

The Ford Edsel is the best remembered example of an industrial–market mis-match. Unilateral nuclear disarmament is Labour's Edsel. It springs from the deep and noble feelings that come naturally to an idealistic party. Gaitskell confronted it, Wilson navigated round it, Callaghan ignored it, Foot proclaimed it and Kinnock has to clear up the mess. In 1983, nuclear weapons policy ran two contradictory sentences together, a Healey interpretation – negotiate nuclear weapons away – and a Foot one: give them up for nothing. This proved to be devisive, unpopular and ineffective, so in 1987 the party eliminated the Healey escape clause.

Unilateralism has all the hallmarks of sectarianism, none of practical politics. It is a matter of faith: Britain giving up nuclear weapons unilaterally will have little effect on anything. It is unsaleable, for nearly two-thirds of the electorate oppose the idea, and counter-productive, for defence is an area of strong feelings and shorthand thinking – for a generation, the commitment to nuclear weapons is almost instinctive: a national virility symbol that many would keep even if the bombs had to be sent to Moscow by motorcycle messenger. It divides, for a section of the party will not accept it. It embarrasses, and guilt over it makes the party atone by promising to increase expenditure on conventional defence weaponry, a burden that is already too heavy, just to show how respectable and virile it is. It damages the party electorally and in the polls. It puts it on the defensive, involves it in endless argument and explanation on the worst possible ground. Yet its inevitable failure makes the faith stronger. To fail is to be right, reinforcing a desire to work harder – in the wilderness. This is masochism as a political philosophy, a folly urged as a vital element of socialism when it is neither left, nor right, just irrelevant.

Unilateral nuclear disarmament on a 'something for nothing' basis frustrates an ambition that is, in itself, sensible. There is no reason why Britain should be a nuclear power at all, unless Mrs Thatcher harbours a desire to bomb Poland. Unilateralism throws this logic away without reducing the nuclear threat or cutting nuclear arsenals down to the very small number of warheads necessary for deterrence or for furthering negotiations. It ends Labour's search for new approaches such as a comprehensive test-ban treaty or a third zero option on short-range weapons, and would deprive Britain of influence in great power negotiations. How can we further the cause if we opt out of the issue?

Most of all, it reduces the possibility of our participating at all by making a Labour government less likely. Unilateralism brings no votes that are not Labour's anyway, and it alienates many of our traditional voters. Those who urge nuclear disarmament will get more out of a Labour government than they ever could from the Tories, who are building up the British deterrent and hardening Nato attitudes at a time when the superpowers are coming together. CND have nowhere to go so why make such suicidal efforts to win them over? The only saleable and sensible proposition must be to put Britain behind all the processes of nuclear arms reduction by putting its own arms into the negotiations, ready to scrap them in return for bigger concessions from the other side. The outcome will be a more secure world and a more effective British contribution to a security that must be collective to work. Labour has struggled to avoid this policy, at a very real cost. Now it is forced to endure a civil war for peace and waste years walking backwards out of a commitment that was unnecessary in the first place.

That issue illustrates Labour's problem. It should formulate policy by balancing between the needs of government, practically and popularity. Yet Labour takes account of only the preferences of its own members, usually as measured by block votes. Nor can it fix priorities. Some unpopular burdens must be espoused by any party of principle determined on change. Yet too many break backs. Even Jesus Christ could carry only one cross and it did not do Him much good, but Labour shoulders all it can find and ends up selling the wrong product, by the wrong techniques, to the wrong market. Its class appeal was once directed at the right mass market: the majority of an electorate motivated by class and economic interest. Brand loyalty was then the key to sales, channel loyalty to viewing, group loyalties to life. Today's sales problem is more complex because conditioned responses motivate fewer people, and those pried loose must be approached with appeals relevant to their lives and instincts, not ours.

Labour must reconcile the unreconcilable by helping the growing sub-class while, at the same time, winning support from the affluent majority; concentrating on economic issues while appealing to an electorate interested in a wider range of secondary issues. Rather than building up a huge mass of policy through our propensity to bumper-sticker politics, the aim should be vagueness, the emphasis on values. President Reagan's 'aw shucks' niceness avoided issues and hard edges, and in the politics of advertising, image and mood manipulation, Labour can learn lessons from his and Margaret's own reality manipulators. The party pitch must encompass image, personnel and policy, not just stir automatic loyalties. It must go straight to the individual, not via the group, and speak about common ground, not sectional loyalties. It has to be general, not specific, for today's aspirations are internationalized and the external signposts are confusing and people want to be talked to as individuals not bits of something else.

Political decisions are being taken as consumers make their choices, some impulsively, some thoughtfully, some reluctantly, some by conditioning, but all in their own way receiving the signals and wondering, 'Will this suit me?', 'What will it do for me?' A campaign is neither a policy exhibition nor an ideological jamboree but a marketing operation for a total product.

Left–Right Scale (Gallup, 1988)

In political matters, people talk of 'the Left' and 'the Right'. How would you place your views on this scale?

		1988	1987
Far left		2	2
Substantially left		3	3
Moderately left		15	10
Slightly left		12	11
	ALL	32	26
Slightly right		15	15
Moderately right		21	24
Substantially right		5	5
Far right		2	3
	ALL	43	47
Middle of the road		10	9
Don't know		14	17

The impressions that carry force come from the television, today's main source of news, information and attitudes. From it, people form their images of the parties and those involved in them. That should benefit Labour, with its powerful front bench, rather than the stupid party with its nonentities, but the gain is minimal because Labour leaders talk two languages: one for the public, one for the party.

Communication must now concentrate on Labour as a product, appealing on all levels to all kinds of buyers. Broad, common attitudes, conditioned by class, have broken down into unconnected clusters so policy tensions within every individual pull in different directions. Society is more pluralistic, individuals more cross pressured. They are more in need of individual persuasion to clarify. So Labour's job would be easier if it were to navigate rather than affronting, and if it were to drop the preoccupation with Left and Right, which brings a perpetual need to pose for the Left. The electorate does not think in those terms. When asked to do so, it professes to be Right rather than Left, but dislikes extremes, especially ours. The majority may be prepared to jump through the 'Left–Right' hoops but most do so with no real

'The Britain we would like to see' (MORI, August 1988)

Labour		Thatcherism	
A mainly socialist society in which public interests and a more controlled economy are most important	49%	A mainly capitalist society in which private interests and free enterprise are most important	43%
A society that emphasizes the social and collective provision of welfare	55%	A society where the individual is encouraged to look after him/herself	40%
A society that emphasizes keeping people at work even where this is not very efficient	42%	A society that emphasizes increasing efficiency rather than keeping people in work	50%
A society that emphasizes similar incomes and rewards for everyone	43%	A society that allows people to make and keep as much as they can	53%
A society in which caring for others is more highly rewarded	79%	A society in which the creation of wealth is more highly rewarded	16%

feeling; they just pretend to be that way, to please the interviewer.

The dimension is no guide to policy. 'Left' is a retirement home for those grown old in the politics of the past. Labour is neither left nor right but a peoples' party. It needs neither a comprehensive ideology nor postures, but knowledge of the people and their aspirations.

People expect to be heard but elect politicians and governments on the basis of their values. For them, public attitudes are common sense, 'win some, lose some'. Only the unrealistic expect to get everything they happen to believe in because most do not believe strongly in anything very much, though they may put themselves in boxes for pollsters. They are unsympathetic to some of Labour's views but like rather more of them than they do the Tories'. They have egalitarian instincts, and 72 per cent think that income gaps are too wide. They do not want to pull down the rich, but are against over-rewarding them. They dislike nationalized monoliths, but are

Privatization vs Nationalization (Gallup, February 1989)

1. Some industries today are in private hands and some are nationalized, owned by the government. What do you think of the present combination of public and private ownership?

More should be privatized/sold off	20
About right	38
More should be nationalized/in public ownership	32
Don't know	11

2. Do you think it would be a good idea or a bad idea if the government decided to sell any of the following nationalized industries by offering shares to the general public and private companies?

	Good idea	Bad idea	Don't know
Electricity	22	68	10
Coal Board	32	56	12
Steel	35	49	16
Water	15	75	10
British Rail	36	53	11

suspicious of big private ones, accept some forms of privatization, but oppose that of water or electricity. They are conservative on the whole but not immutable. This government's unbalanced enthusiasm for markets and inequality has moved the electorate the other way. Compared to the Europeans', British public opinion was previously hard-hearted and unsympathetic, blaming unemployment and poverty on those who suffered from it, but now ten years of Thatcherism have warmed a few cockles.

Because the government has pursued prejudice to perverse conclusions, Labour's policy problem is on the way to being solved. It is now the government that is out of line with the public agenda, and which is felt to be the weakest on most things except the economy and inflation, and both of these will change with failure. People take their cue about which party is the best to deal with problems from their general perception of those parties. On the basis of government performance, Labour is doing better, a situation that can be improved by hard work. Not outlandish policy commitments, but activity, public concern and a show of effort and commitment; being

Changes in Britain (Gallup, 1987)

We would like your views on some of the general changes that have been taking place in Britain over the last few years.

	1987	1981
The welfare benefits that are available today?		
Gone much too far	6	11
Gone a little too far	10	14
About right	26	36
Not gone quite far enough	30	21
Not gone nearly far enough	21	12
Don't now	6	6
Moves to go easier on people who break the law?		
Gone much too far	22	21
Gone a little too far	18	18
About right	12	13
Not gone quite far enough	24	23
Not gone nearly far enough	20	19
Don't know	4	6
People showing less respect for authority?		
Gone much too far	35	35
Gone a little too far	24	26
About right	13	13
Not gone quite far enough	16	11
Not gone nearly far enough	7	8
Don't know	4	7
Recent attempts to ensure equality for minority groups in Britain?		
Gone much too far	14	12
Gone a little too far	15	13
About right	31	38
Not gone quite far enough	20	20
Not gone nearly far enough	10	11
Don't know	11	7

seen to be working at policy rather than actually unveiling reams of it; offering responsive policies to answer strong concerns rather than confronting them.

It must also decide what issues it wants to concentrate on and which are best left to the other side. There is no sense in

	1987	1981
The change towards modern methods in teaching children at school nowadays?		
Gone much too far	16	19
Gone a little too far	18	19
About right	27	26
Not gone quite far enough	14	12
Not gone nearly far enough	9	5
Don't know	15	19
The reduction of Britain's military strength?		
Gone much too far	14	21
Gone a little too far	18	20
About right	34	23
Not gone quite far enough	13	11
Not gone nearly far enough	10	12
Don't know	11	13
Attempts to ensure quality for women?		
Gone much too far	5	4
Gone a little too far	6	8
About right	40	51
Not gone quite far enough	27	19
Not gone nearly far enough	15	12
Don't know	6	6

trying to outdo the Tories on military strength, though every reason to avoid the appearance of weakness. Labour must use indications and resonances rather than hard-and-fast commitments. That means assessing where it is weak and doing something about it. For example, Labour's strength is spending – on jobs, education, welfare – but these are offered to an electorate that wants contradictory things, and expects efficiency and economy. So the party must concentrate on broad values, dilute specifics, find out what the majority want and feed it back to them, concentrating on good intentions and willingness to listen, and sending signals by shows of concern or even innuendo rather than making everything explicit.

The best guide to sales is the market research of opinion polls. Conservatives exploit them to map out approaches, understand the electorate and delineate stepping stones on the

Best Party (MORI, June 1987)

I am going to read out a list of problems facing Britain today. I would like you to tell me whether you think the Conservative Party, the Labour Party or the Liberal/SDP Alliance has the best policies on each problem.

	Start of election		End		Change
	%	%	%	%	
Unemployment					
Conservative	27	28	33	30	+3
Labour	35	34	34	35	0
Liberal/SDP Alliance	16	17	19	20	+4
Don't know/none	22	21	15	15	−7
Education/schools					
Conservative	31	33	32	30	−1
Labour	29	30	33	33	+4
Liberal/SDP Alliance	17	17	19	21	+4
Don't know/none	23	20	15	15	−8
National Health Service					
Conservative	24	24	27	27	+3
Labour	42	42	41	40	−2
Liberal/SDP Alliance	15	16	18	20	+5
Don't know/none	19	18	14	13	−6
Defence generally					
Conservative	48	49	52	50	+2
Labour	21	22	23	24	+3
Liberal/SDP Alliance	13	14	15	16	+3
Don't know/none	18	15	10	9	−9
Law and order					
Conservative	45	42	43	43	−2
Labour	18	22	25	25	+7
Liberal/SDP Alliance	11	12	15	15	+4
Don't know/none	26	23	17	17	−9
Housing					
Conservative	28	31	34	33	+5
Labour	39	38	37	39	0
Liberal/SDP Alliance	10	12	15	15	+5
Don't know/none	23	19	13	13	−10
Inflation					
Conservative	56	57	57	58	+2

	Start of election		End		Change
	%	%	%	%	
Labour	16	20	22	21	+ 5
Liberal/SDP Alliance	8	8	10	11	+ 3
Don't know/none	19	15	11	10	− 9
Disarmament					
Conservative	38	38	44	43	+ 5
Labour	30	29	27	28	− 2
Liberal/SDP Alliance	14	17	16	19	+ 5
Don't know/none	18	16	12	11	− 7
Trade unions					
Conservative	36	39	40	41	+ 5
Labour	36	37	37	38	+ 2
Liberal/SDP Alliance	8	8	10	11	+ 3
Don't know/none	19	16	13	10	− 9

way to power. Labour must, too: understanding the world through ideology would mean finding the way south using 1926 Ordnance Survey maps. Market research must also be fed into policy process so that the popularity of policies can be taken into account, not stumbled across on the doorstep. Labour might once have been able to speak for the workers. Now it must pay to find out what they think because it cannot get it for free by telepathy or block vote.

In market politics, the brand loyal can be taken for granted. The appeal is pitched at those to be won. Labour has usually done the opposite but must now speak to those who it needs, not any specific group, whether it be defined as yuppy, skilled, young, female or middle class, but the universe of people who inhabit the middle ground. They are easily frightened by extremism. They want indications of concern and intention rather than long shopping lists, particularly in areas where their own lives are affected because they want a government and a party on their side.

Change in attitudes comes partly by reaction. The Conservatives came in on the populist ticket of cutting taxes, always a popular strategy even among those who do not pay any. The failure to feel any substantial benefit from this process has coupled with the deterioration in the quality of services to produce the reaction against the Tories. In the British Social Attitudes surveys, the proportion wanting more taxes to finance spending on health, education and social benefits, 31 per cent in 1983, went up to 46 per cent in 1986. By 1988, Gallup was showing that only 11 per cent of their national sample wanted taxes cut at the expense of some reduction in government services such as health, education and welfare, 19 per cent wanted things left as they were, but two-thirds thought that services such as health, education and welfare should be extended, even if it meant some increases in taxes. That feeling was not strong, but it symbolized a change in the popular mood, part of that great shift that ultimately changes everything.

The shift was confirmed by reactions to the budget. MORI showed that most people supported cuts in the standard rate of tax but were opposed to cutting the higher rate. They felt that the budget was unfair and socially divisive. By pushing his priorities too far, and too fast, Nigel Lawson had accelerated a shift that was already underway.

Perceptions of parties are largely instrumental, impressions of success or failure, competence or weakness, unity or disunity. These crystallize through the impact of economic performance on lives and expectations. The views of the public, though clearly influenced by the media, are not unrealistic, as Gallup's questions on the Labour Party show.

Labour's key weakness is not policy but its position on instrumental issues. The Thatcher government is more extreme than any that has gone before, but Labour is the one that is seen as extremist. Labour was viewed in the 1960s as more united than the Tories. Now it is considered disunited, even a nest of extremists. In 1987, 40 per cent of Labour 'identifiers' who voted for another party gave Labour's extremism and disunity as their reasons for switching.

The basis on which electors make their assessments is delivery. More well-being – up goes the government's standing. More misery, particularly unemployment – down it goes. The correlation is clear with the 'confidence index': questions on whether economic conditions will stay the same or get worse over the next 12 months. Optimism means poll success, which is why this government has been so popular for so long, and

Reasons for Not Voting Labour (Gallup, July 1988)

	Today	October 1987
Trade unions have too much control of the Labour Party	39	35
Labour's too divided	39	34
I can't see Neil Kinnock as prime minister	37	31
Labour's defence policy is dangerous	34	39
Labour has moved too far to the left	30	34
Labour's in the hands of extremists	23	25
I don't know what Labour stands for any more	23	20
Taxes would go up under a Labour government	22	27
Labour governments can't control inflation	22	26
I will be personally worse off under Labour	19	21
I disagree with Labour's stand on privatization	19	18
Labour's too concerned about helping minorities	18	19
I've never voted Labour and see no reason for changing now	18	15
The real interest of the workers aren't what Labour is about today	16	18
I don't know who's in charge of the Labour Party today	12	13
There's too much secrecy in the Labour Party today	12	11
None of these	21	20

why the Conservatives have had a lead on the issue of 'who makes Britain more prosperous', with 52 per cent saying 'Conservative' and 23 per cent 'Labour'. Oil has given the government the ability to avoid the political and economic crises that other political flesh has been heir to.

The results of that success can be seen in the mid-1988 tables from MORI. At that stage, most people were content, but this was to be undermined by Nigel Lawson's great deflation. Economic confidence as evinced by the MORI poll has duly fallen from a positive 15 per cent in May 1988 to a negative 24 per cent at the turn of the year. As deflation bites, Labour can plant its seeds of discontent, while Lawson destroys the image of success and competence that has been crucial, ending the prosperity that has underpinned everything.

Economic Satisfaction (MORI, August 1988)
The things people can buy and do – their housing, furniture, food, cars, recreation and travel – make up their standard of living. How satisfied or dissatisfied do you feel about your standard of living at present?

	All %	Con %	Lab %	SLD/ SDP %
Very satisfied	16	22	9	17
Fairly satisfied	58	64	52	66
Fairly dissatisfied	10	6	15	3
Very dissatisfied	8	2	15	3
Neither/don't know/no opinion	8	6	9	11

Overall, do you think your present standard of living is higher, lower or about the same as five years ago?

Higher	42	53	30	45
Lower	27	18	38	21
About the same	30	29	31	32
Don't know	1	*	1	1
Net higher	+ 15	+ 25	− 8	+ 24

And do you think it will be higher, lower or about the same in five years' time?

Higher	35	48	24	31
Lower	23	11	34	27
About the same	33	33	33	35
Don't know	8	8	9	7
Net higher	+ 12	+ 37	− 10	+ 4

The degree to which this helps us is largely in our own hands, for to seize the initiative from a deadlocked Alliance and connect economic failure with a general picture of government failure will give us the impetus to ride forward on.

Labour believes in commitment and policies. The essence of media politics is impression and image. To this end, we must show concern continuously but avoid commitments that can be taken down and used in evidence against us. The art was demonstrated in 1952 by Eisenhower in his famous TV slots. 'Mamie tells me she's worried about rising prices,' Ike announced. 'When I get to Washington, I'm going to do something about that.' Policies do not win elections, and a manifesto is a platform from which to board a train, not something to be taken, every brick of it, on the journey. Rather it is an expression of a party's values and concerns: broad intentions not details, hopes not specifics. The art of coarse trap-shutting is one that Labour could learn for no policy can suit every hope in every breast. However, we can show ourselves to be in tune with the broad aspirations of society: sympathetic, concerned, thoughtful, preoccupied with people.

Parties bidding for power must absorb the mood of the time. Hitherto, the Conservatives have had to adjust more than Labour, accepting the world Labour built from 1945 to 1951, the mixed economy, Keynesian management and a measure of redistribution. Now it is Labour's turn to accept new norms, a transformation that will be easier in power as it has been in Spain and Australasia. Yet from 1976 to 1979, when the Callaghan government introduced monetarism, cut spending and sold shares in BP, it did it in a shamefaced and embarrassed fashion rather than opting for the boldness that could have wrongfooted Tory opponents and given Labour a new lease of life.

That transition to backing efficiency, markets, deregulation and competition must now be made in opposition with the party outside Parliament stronger. Times are harder, money is shorter and efficiency is essential, although inefficiency never was part of socialism. So we have to accept the new terms of the debate. Controls and monoliths are unpopular, and people are suspicious of the restrictive and protective faces of Labour, doubtful about their efficiency and critical of big-spending socialism and its 'handouts', 'scroungers' and hangers-on. The emphasis must therefore be on efficient spending that can be justified by a return in better service, jobs and fairness, subjecting all, including our friends, to the tests of efficiency and effectiveness, rather than protecting some, as the Conservatives have done with the professions, the City, the banks and the rest of their supporters.

This transformation accepts those elements of Thatcherism that the public have welcomed, but adds a new dimension – 'soul' – to efficiency. This will give the market a human face by putting individuals and their rights to services and support at the centre, managing markets for people, not brute impersonal forces. This new element was lacking in 1983, when we were sulking, and in 1987, when we dare not say anything too loudly. It must now be pursued boldly: Labour is better, more efficient, smarter, but it really cares, too. Unlike Mrs Thatcher, it has a heart.

The mood is turned against the government by amplifying the problems that Thatcherism is author of, and to which the market has no solution: soaring house prices, the housing crisis, strained services, grinding poverty, crowded roads and railways, the crumbling health service, collapsing sewers, the shabby public sector, the greedy profits and impersonality of British Telecom, British Gas and the Electricity Board, the extravagant lifestyles of the City and the rich, the death of industries and jobs, the polluted environment. Responsibility falls on this government and Labour can provide answers.

'Let's get better with Labour' does not mean the reversal of every change carried out by Mrs Thatcher and her cronies, but a caring and sensitive approach to replace casual brutality and endless lecturing. As the economy stagnates with Nigel Lawson's great deflation, expansion will be our alternative. No miracles but a concerted effort to rebuild national strength and an economy that gives the people the basics of jobs, growth and the ability to control their world. The market is not fair, and public opinion is not enamoured of it, so put people at the centre and manage it for them. The social and health services and education are all shabby and run down, so concentrate on generating the wealth to improve them. Liberating growth means low interest rates and devaluation but 'cheap money', rhetoric about taking power from the merchants of greed and talk of a 'competitive currency' sound so much better.

As the economy fails, the feeling will grow that selfishness has 'gone too far'. The nation will want a shift in all the social balances that Mrs Thatcher has tilted her way. People need to be elevated over money by populist, anti-bank campaigning to make money the servant, not the master. Imports are felt to be a threat, and there is even majority support for import controls and a general feeling that British industry should be helped to rebuild. So by shifting the balances, rather than scrapping and starting again, we will be doing what parties must by working with the popular grain.

To counter the crude populism of the right – the dark side of everyone – there is a noble and traditional populism of the heart that Labour has never tapped: the feelings that humans are proximate to God, that every valley should be exalted, the mountains laid low, that *aller Menschen werden Bruder* – we are one of another, every child has a prospect and deserves a chance, every person has the seeds of redemption within him or her, Jack's as good as his master – while the mighty should be pulled down from their thrones, and the monoliths reduced to human scale. All these are a part of British conditioning. Tapping the wellsprings of such instincts while offering an alternative to failed selfishness should allow Labour to proclaim the better side of populism and counter the sulky side that Margaret Thatcher has made her own.

That instinct can also be articulated through the attack on privilege that comes naturally to a classless party, opposed to both wealth and class. Labour has not exploited this natural stance because it is also a protective party defending the privileges of unions, public-sector workers and 'left' vested interests. Yet a radical egalitarian stance is believable only if universally applied. That means competition among solicitors, doctors, estate agents and barristers to turn the professions into service industries rather than allowing them to remain self-serving conspiracies against the public – and genuine competition not just Tory money-saving. It means boosting the consumer and an attack on the privileges of wealth and the boardroom so lavishly increased by this government, on the privileges and exclusivity of public schools, on the unions and the corrupt, self-serving 'self-regulation' of the City, the financial community and the privatized monoliths, on the state itself. There is a universe of perks and privileges from which the majority are excluded. Attacking it will garner support and further Labour's cause, as well as those of fairness and efficiency.

All these are useful themes. Yet the main unifying theme is an attack, not on Margaret Thatcher personally, but on a government that will not listen – a crusade for fairness. Politics is a weatherhouse. As the nasty woman retreats, the nice, smiling man emerges. The mood changes, as mysteriously and almost as totally as it changed the other way. So Labour's job is to give impetus and an intellectual and policy gloss to the shift. Working with the grain means an appeal to the basic values overlain in the Thatcherite hegemony, advancing them not as party values but as a basis for unity, on which all the forces opposed to the present minority rule can stand. Fairness is the frontline.

Oppositions must calculate who to win over. Two groups are vital: the workers who left us, attracted by Mrs Thatcher's bold, confident promises to make things better; and the liberal middle-class element, who left in despair at Labour's folly. The first require fairness, competence and practical policies for jobs and economic growth. They will be drawn back as the prosperity that underpins Thatcherism fails. With the second group, Labour needs to devise a policy of empowerment. Mrs Thatcher's exercise in will has frustrated the widespread desire of everyone to 'be someone', to be heard, to be listened to and consulted, to have a say and to be able to make things happen – in short, to feel empowered. While talking of setting the people free, the Prime Minister has made them more subject to employers and the merchants of greed and to herself bossing them about at some length. People who are more vulnerable in her harder, colder world, long for both the comfort of community and greater control over their own destinies, their work, their environment, the services they get, both public and private.

Empowerment means passing power to the people and focusing their antagonisms against a system that has failed. That approach paid large dividends for the French Socialists in 1981 with '*auto-gestion*'. It will work, too, for us because of the accumulated frustration. We can set the people free in a way that Mrs Thatcher never could: by providing a platform for them to shape their own destinies and by bringing democracy closer, to give them the influence and involvement, the ability to be heard, that they want. That can make them citizens, no longer subjects of the imperial Queen. This theme is universal in its appeal. So is a massive expansion of education and its opportunities, of training and technology, a commitment to research and development, re-skilling, re-educating, re-training the community. That unites both middle class and skilled workers, as well as being what we must do to survive in a competitive world where our only strengths now are our neglected people.

The basic theme that will unite all the others is Britain become a nation again. The British are peculiar in many ways but most of all in lacking the clear sense of national identity that other nations have. This sense of identity has always been fragmented by class, a sense of us and them rather than us, and has been focussed on institutions, particularly the myth of the Crown in Parliament. Now both are fading as class instincts weaken and institutions, even the show biz monarchy, are less respected. So the nation is left with no sense of being, togetherness or identity, merely negative instincts and festering resentments. The latent, proud instincts of nationalism have been betrayed by decades of futile failure, the long decline into the Common Market, the growing frustration at being left behind. It emerged during the Falklands dispute. It is why British nuclear weapons are popular. The polls indicate a dislike of decline, a feeling that Mrs Thatcher has not built the nation's strength, that Britain counts for less, and should count for more. There is a harvest of votes awaiting a party that encourages and focuses these latent instincts into a collective effort to rebuild the nation and its pride.

Yet nationalism is a card that Labour plays uneasily. Our instincts are internationalist; we fear populism. All this is perverse, for Labour is the only party of the nation representing those who cannot leave, export their capital, or flog themselves on the international market, those who are proudest of being British, and most baffled in their loyalty. It is the natural party of national reconstruction, its aim a strong economy. So it should throw off its *naïveté* and get down to the people with a patriotic approach, dedicated to making Britain strong again, a nation that catches up with the rest of the world instead of limping behind, and can hold its head high because it has the economic strength and the quality of life and services of a great country. The party that drapes itself in the Union Jack and fights on a platform of national pride not only taps deep well-springs but fills a gaping void in British politics. Indeed it can also mobilize the subordinate nationalisms of this disunited kingdom, with policies of regional independence and devolution not just for Scotland but all the component regions.

'Self-rule for everyone' taps Scottish pride as well as the unreasonably neglected regional feelings of Yorkshire, the North-east, the West Midlands and Wales, and to offer this in the context of a strong, proud Britain unifies them all.

By striking such instinctive chords, Labour can give its attack on a failed government a resonance and a nobler dimension. Yet parties have to be multi-ring circuses, appealing to different tastes, needing clowns as well as high seriousness, hucksters as well as theorists. The baits and lures in which the basic themes should be decked out can also further our basic values, expansion and fairness, by developing an electorally attractive spending package designed to stimulate demand by those who spend it most quickly. Allow those who have lived in council housing for twenty years to live rent free. Give free bus passes, off-peak rail travel, and television licences to pensioners, and a better deal to 'victims of Thatcher' through cash benefits for the long-term unemployed and single parent families. Help first-time buyers with low and middling incomes by redistributing mortgage tax relief their way, by giving cash grants and enabling them to capitalize child benefit for a number of years ahead so that they can put down deposits. The Tories will cry 'who's going to pay for it?' but their council house raffles, privatization bribes, tax cuts and, in 1983, the increase in mortgage tax relief just before the election have all shown the way, and at much greater expense than the aforementioned socially beneficial proposals.

The third ring of the circus is high seriousness. People view political parties as bodies dedicated to a purpose. They want to know that the party they pick can supply what they want and judge it as an instrument able to act for them. It must be competent, serious and dedicated to their interests not to its own preoccupations and obsessions. Government dominates such assessments because of the impact that policies can have on lives. Electors who turned past governments out were effectively ratifying a collapse, a burn-out, a loss of the way, that had already occurred. Yet the same judgement is also applied to the opposition and it is conditioned partly by the weatherhouse effect, partly by an objective assessment. As the government's standing declines, people will be looking ever more critically at Labour, evaluating it as a potential government. At the moment Labour is shedding its extremist image and emerging as the only party which can turn out the government. It is, however, still weak on leadership (67 per cent find it 'poor'), disunity (71 per cent say 'too split') and competence (41 per cent find it competent as against 77 per cent for the Conservatives). All are crucial influences, for in consumer politics people 'buy' parties because of their instrumental appeal, and the best buy is the one that seems better able to do the job. By the 1990s the electorate will want a strong nation, a system with heart, dedication to caring values and hence a party that shows those concerns and looks competent enough to do something about them. That means projecting Labour's able and effective team as the superior alternative to Maggie and the Minions. It means a serious, dedicated and united party, proferring attractive policies to make the nation strong again, earnest in its policy process rather than boring the nation to death with every detail, projecting the confidence that knowing it has the answers gives rise to.

People do not expect all the answers. They are now as suspicious of blazing certainty as they once were of tricky-dickery and are certainly ready to welcome a little humility. Yet they do want a party to look like a party, to inspire confidence as a party, and to seem competent to govern the nation. None of this is gimmickry, intellectual prostitution or irrelevant ideology. It is just the deeply serious business of being a political party rather than an Outward Bound course in play-way politics.

9
Future Conditional

Wider still and wider shall Labour's bounds be set. Blander still and broader shall Labour's policies get. Such is the prescription for reversing decline and transforming a sect into a broad people's party. Less a tight disciplined body than a broad rally for change, reaching out to make contact with every heart and impress every head, putting Labour into communion once again with the nation it aspires to rebuild. This is not betrayal but realism, and it is an exciting challenge to adjust to a new nation and build a broad coalition for progress. The old betterment, pursued in a new world, in ways calculated to bring the Thatcher aberration to an early end, will make Labour once again the political expression of the great majority of this nation.

The changes must be made, and some are being made, but they will not be enough. The revolutions in organization, policy and ideology are goals, archetypes to aim at, but a mite difficult for a conservative party to achieve in the two years that remain before the election. This government has put down deep roots. Those locked into the old find it difficult to leap in one bound on to the new and be free. So Labour must complement that essential programme by embracing another agenda as well. It must now think the unthinkable: it has to work with all the other political forces excluded from the hegemony of the Right. People of goodwill, liberal spirits, humanitarians, progressives, environmentalists – the whole panopoly of pluralism brought together into a new political relationship, for the limited but paramount objective: of ending the Thatcher counter-revolution. To do that, Labour must also consider change in an electoral system that excludes us, and them, from power.

The second change is a concomitant of the first, the one is

impossible without the other. Yet thanks to the unique situation that Margaret Thatcher has created, it now becomes possible to manoeuvre in such a way as to get both, or neither, or one with or without the benefits of the other. Here, if nowhere else, Labour is free to decide. We call the shots; if we have the imagination to see them.

The party of liberty, equality and fraternity should naturally embrace an electoral system that is democratic, makes votes more equal and binds the community together. That system is proportional representation (PR). The party that wants an irreversible transfer of power to working people cannot get it in our present electoral system, for everything is reversible, and much of it has now been reversed. Indeed in this system it is increasingly difficult to get power at all. Unfortunately policy somersaults are possible only for the Tories. Labour has to adjust more slowly. It now can, although it must do so by replacing its old, failed majoritarian triumphalism with party cooperation, which, with PR, opens up a new world and new opportunities. Labour has to accept some part of this process because that is the hard reality in which it must work.

Change in the electoral system and a willingness to work with other parties go together. The second may be easier than the first, if only because we have already done it, but here they must be considered the other way round, because it is the electoral system that has amplified Labour's self-inflicted damage and distanced it from power. Just as the present system boosts majorities, so it compounds decline, relegating Labour to a sectional minority of the kind that could have a political impact under proportional representation but is impotent under 'first past the post'. The system has, therefore, enthroned the dictatorship of the minority, leaving Labour railing impotently, a voice in the wilderness of the North, Scotland and Wales, the best parts of the country, the worst of the electoral balance.

Few other advanced democracies combine Britain's centralized political system and powerful executive with a 'winner takes all' electoral system based on single-member constituencies. Canada, Australia and the United States combine 'first past the post' with a federal system, fragmenting power and making the central government less crucial: an Aussie

'Thatch' could not come the raw prawn on the states. Most European countries have proportional representation, basing Parliaments on the political preferences of the people, stopping the winner taking all by making coalition and consultation essential and spreading power. France has alternated between electoral systems, but even its current 'first past the post' system has run-off elections ensuring, like the Australian system of listed preferences, that elected candidates at least have a majority in their own constituency.

Only Britain has an elective dictatorship built on an undemocratic electoral system and sustained by party control of the legislature. The question that Labour, and the country, must face is whether an electoral system is not tyrannical when it puts the machinery of the world's most powerful executive into the hands of a freak minority, and then makes it difficult either to turn that minority out, or to allow the wishes of the people to prevail. Has it now outlived its usefulness?

The main argument for proportional representation is fairness. Our system is government by party. Therefore, the party preferences of the electorate should be reflected in the legislature to give everyone a stake in the result, instead of throwing most choices on the scrap heap, and creating strong government by disenfranchising most electors. People whose votes make little contribution to the result feel no commitment to it. This generates the negative feelings that are so powerful a feature of British politics. The vote has been fought for over generations yet we treat it as a lottery in which most tickets are worthless.

No one can build a democratic superstructure on an undemocratic base. Both major parties justify and defend the system, but that says more about the strength of vested interest than about any objective assessment of the needs of democracy. Indeed, such a defence is contemptuous of real people because it panders to the selfish interests of parties, and, today, really only of one – the Conservatives. The implicit argument is that the system may be unfair, it may produce indefensible results, but it makes sense to the major parties because they are either in power or hope to be next time. Three election defeats in a row should lead Labour to reconsider. If it does not, it is because some see the present electoral system as all that stops Labour going down the plug-hole of history.

What does Labour get out of a system that provides strong government but only to the Conservatives, and it doles out lemons to us? In 1983, Mrs Thatcher won an increased number of seats on a falling vote, achieving (in every election since 1979) a dictatorial majority with most people voting against her. She did this because the electoral system and the social base of politics are now out of adjustment. That failure hits Labour, not the Conservatives. System and society meshed well enough together in the immediate post-war period when the electorate was stable and the electoral system could magnify a small shift in votes into a bigger shift of seats to provide strong government. Now there are half the number of marginal seats than there were in the 1950s and the government is more difficult to turn out.

Margaret Thatcher is an enthusiastic supporter of the present electoral system. She would not be in power without it. By winning just 43 per cent of the vote, and appealing to around a third of the electorate, she was able to put together a majority of over 100. Whether it would make the same sense to Labour is a different question. Labour was originally committed to PR, but in more recent years, the party has refused even to consider it. At the 1987 annual conference, after a managed debate and a negative speech from Roy Hattersley, who concentrated on clobbering the SDP rather than on the future, the party decided to keep its head in the sand. It refused to think about the possibilities that PR might hold for Labour.

Labour people support the present electoral system because they want the same chance to apply their own follies as the Tories have done. 'We will be the masters – eventually' is the mentality. It is unhealthy and irrational for, under this electoral system, Labour has only won two elections – in 1945 and 1966 – with a majority of more than ten. Real majorities go to the Tories, and the opposition cannot now turn out the government unless the government cooperates by a prolonged bout of folly, or a spot of political suicide. As the party of fairness, we have usually given this help to our opponents when in power, most spectacularly in 1979. Some Tory governments have also played fair. It took the first post-war Tory government 13 years to decompose but Ted Heath perfected the art in four. Margaret Thatcher, unfortunately, has no such selfless devotion to being fair to lame oppositions. In the face of such realities, Labour's attachment to an electoral system that defeats it is really a symptom of intellectual rigor mortis, or of its eternal preference for being right, pure and in opposition for ever.

In this electoral system, opposition's task is nearly impossible. There are no cavalry on the horizon, just more Indians. The Boundary Commission will be re-activated in 1991 and will report in 1993 or 1994 in time for the election after next. Since the last redistribution, the three-fifths of the nation that gave Mrs Thatcher a majority has grown, Labour's two-fifths has shrunk. The mainly Tory Shire counties have an increased population of 2.6 million, the mainly Labour metropolitan counties have lost 60,000, the London boroughs 160,000. Any redistribution that takes account of this will lose Labour ten seats and add ten to the Tory column, so that Labour will come to the 1996 election with an automatic deficit of 20 seats before the television screen has even flickered. Since no commentator has suggested a Labour majority as big as 20 in 1991, the case for Labour to espouse a new electoral system quickly is the equivalent of avoiding a deathbed repentance.

Labour must, therefore, consider a new electoral system, and with it 'proportional politics', which will allow it to play a far more useful part than now. Under PR, the Left can have majority governments, as it has in Sweden and Spain. It always tries to win a majority but can get it only with a majority of voters, which is not Labour's position at the moment. So in the immediate present it would have to work with others to get power under PR just as it probably does under 'first past the post'. Yet at least power would then be available to us where it is not under 'first past the post'. The choice is, therefore, a straight one: work for power or sulk. Under PR, power is available at the end of the hard work; under 'first past the post', it is problematical for under-parties. The only change Labour is required to make is an acceptance of reality the better to seize opportunity. Labour must for it has become so reduced that there is no alternative to learning the techniques and espousing the framework of cooperation and sharing. We may not like coalition and the polls indicate that the public is not keen particularly since David Owen gave it a bad name. Yet if the wish of the nation is that parties should work together, they have no right to stand in the way and put themselves first.

The challenge for Labour is to throw away the trappings of the present system and make a contribution to the future, instead of being crushed under Margaret Thatcher's coronation coach. Labour can be socialist, unregenerate, brave and defiant, making no compromise with the electorate as it fades away into history. Yet even here it faces a paradox. Only PR allows such a sectional party to achieve anything by giving it a useful role – as many seats as now – plus influence as a player. Our system relegates it. Labour's choice is not therefore between change and not changing but in getting a return on the change it has to make anyway or not. With 'first past the post', change means dilution, blandness and broader appeals to add more votes to the traditional core, and the probability of doing all that for nothing. With PR, it means coalition, compromises and deals, to add enough other party votes and seats to whatever it can win on its own, by working with another party or parties to hold office and wield power. Our European brother parties have all made their choice – for PR. It should be ours too, for we would have more certain results and a greater bonus in seats and influence, in return for less dilution.

The assumption is that PR would benefit only the third party. However, because it would make politics healthier and more rational, it would be better for Labour, and might even reduce the third party to a more realistic level. The Liberals have had a high vote because, in this electoral system, they provide the opportunity to voters to make a harmless protest without substantial consequences – a bucket to spit into, a safety valve. In proportional representation, every vote is a wanted vote, it has an effect on government and must be considered not thrown away. Voting is evaluated differently. Negative factors would be less important, and people would have to assess whether they want the third party in government and why. On that basis, a party of escapist fantasies, one that stands in the middle of every road like a long yellow streak littered with dead skunks, would be less attractive and relevant than a party with a firm base on which to build to power. The two major parties would still be the basic players. Democrat seats would be in proportion to votes. Their votes would be fewer.

Proportional representation holds out other benefits for Labour. It would be forced to transform its attitudes. Under 'first past the post' as it operated up to 1979, there was a premium on internal power struggles. When elections were decided by reactions against the government, opposition could come into power on the back of that reaction whatever its policies, so the incentive was to struggle for power within the party, to take over its machine and dictate policies, however daft, with which it would win anyway on the negative tide. So the pattern up to 1979 concentrated the efforts of the party in opposition on making Labour truly socialist, to carry socialism into power on the back of the reaction against a Tory incumbent. That was the only conceivable rationale for the power struggle between 1979 and 1983, a struggle that was, in fact, discredited and damaged Labour and eliminated its prospect of power. Little of that agenda of folly could have been done, proposed or even considered under proportional representation for this forces every party to puts its best face, best candidates and most attractive policies forward. Parties have to go out to build up support and educate opinion. They must argue the case with the people, not the party, and are forced to do what should be their real job in consumer democracy. PR puts the electorate first – which is what Labour needs to do.

PR is a rational system that offers scope and opportunity to rational parties. 'First past the post' is negative, encourages irresponsibility and puts a premium on escapism. PR also opens up another opportunity. Labour is presently relegated to the North, Scotland and Wales. There, people are saying by their Labour votes that they are excluded from the prosperity and improvement of the South-east. 'First past the post' locks Labour into these declining areas. It is unable to reach out because it is not viable in huge areas of the South; there,

Labour votes deliver no return in MPs, and little in councillors, because Labour is in third place or irrelevant. The Labour vote drifts away to Democrats in second place who have the only prospect of turning out incumbent Tories. Labour voters turn to apathy, factional follies or despair, or they just grow old and grey, a northern exiles association clustering together to talk about the old days and places. In such areas, Labour is faltering because it is irrelevant. Only a system that delivers a return to all voters will allow Labour to reach out and become a national party again, with members elected everywhere.

Considering PR does not mean getting bogged down into any argument about systems. That is premature. Rather as if the hard task of establishing an abortion clinic in Dublin were stopped because of rows over whether it should use aspiration or surgical methods. The choice between party list, the additional-member system as in West Germany or the single transferable vote as in Ireland does not matter. The system can be chosen to produce the preferred results: a threshold to keep out lunatics; a constituency base; more weight for the parties, or less. All are available if required. Only the principle of proportionality is important at this stage of the argument. To argue the minutiae of systems divides the case and wastes time. All systems of PR would help Labour more than the present one.

Nor will half-measures work. Some new Labour converts to the PR idea look to the 'alternative vote' rather than to PR: a half-baked compromise for a party that loves muddy muddles. Its fault lies in the fact that it is not proportional. Candidates in each individual constituency are listed in order of preference, ensuring a fairer, more respectable result in that constituency, but doing nothing outside it, so it would not help Labour to reach South. It is the politics of the blackball – used in Australia when the Catholic DLP split away from the ALP and cast its second preferences against Labour, keeping the ALP out of power for over a decade. Here, too, Labour is everyone's favourite for the blackball. The press would certainly encourage fear of us while the cuddly Democrats, the soft middle, would be everyone's favourite second preference. The alternative vote would boost them but do nothing for Labour. Those who have gone so far as to have taken up the alternative vote need to go all the way to PR to fulfil their hopes for change. Meanwhile the increasing numbers in the party who support PR must think about how they can get it. They look to converting the party. They should envisage it as a stepping stone to power.

Now is the time for Labour to open its mind to the possibilities that would arise from PR, and consider whether Labour can achieve anything without it. The thorny problem of how the party evaluates its election prospects will be central. If Labour is defeated in 1991, there will be an explosion of interest in proportional representation, just as there was in constituencies in the South after 1987. Too late. Mrs Thatcher will have yet another term, taking Britain and herself mummified into the mid-1990s. It is vital to win early. So now is the best time to consider PR and to start making plans for a political future that involves it. Early consideration carries the additional bonus that Labour would not even be required to go through the agony of making up its mind on PR, but would rather see its value as part of a strategy for power, preparatory to allowing the electorate to decide the actual issue in the only fair and democratic way. What does have to be considered soon, and at length, is the extent to which Labour should carry on alone – the Sinn Fein of power politics – or work with others.

The Democrats will not go away. We can get a lot of humour out of their internal difficulties, pretend we don't know what to call them, condescend to Paddy Ashdown as Robin without Batman, but their strength and permanence require us to play by different rules. When the third-party vote hovers around 10 per cent, it can be ignored, a mere residual. At higher levels of third-party voting, when it rises to a quarter or a third, and when it wins by-elections and benefits from Labour follies by taking Labour seats – Rochdale, Liverpool, Edgehill, Bermondsey, Greenwich – and building there a base that many electors clearly regard as equivalent to Labour, then the rules change. We are in a different game but competing for the same ground. That means playing for displacement. Destruction is impossible, much as we might pray for it.

The third party has grown from a safety valve for discontent to a threat. We have shrunk. The ratio between the parties is 4:3:2 – no longer a two-party system, nor yet a three-party one. A common view is that the third party in fact helps Labour by syphoning Tory votes and seats into futility. The reverse happened in the early 1950s when Liberal withdrawals in 1951 certainly put Churchill in power, but in 1964, the Liberals took votes almost equally from Labour and the Tories, and in 1974, Labour won not because of the Liberals but through its own strong showing in Tory marginals, especially in the North-west. The only tactical contribution was by Labour voters in a few seats in Scotland going to the Nationalists and a few in England to the Liberals, so depriving Edward Heath of his majority rather than giving seats to Labour. Even if Liberals throw seats to Labour, they would be gains by default, not winning, and would not help Labour's real problem: it is weak in huge areas where it cannot win but needs to. In any case, projecting the 1964 and 1974 vote from those two elections on a declining curve to 1991 offers Labour little hope of becoming even the largest single party. Its vote has slipped and the third-party vote has risen.

The Democrats do not help us; they hinder. A split opposition is far less attractive and less able to replace the incumbent because it puts off those who need to see an alternative before they will turn the government out. The Democrats deprive Labour of the necessary aura of being the inevitable alternative, and of any bandwagon charisma, particularly between elections. Once David Owen's blocking game waged with divisive SDP candidates in by-elections is removed, the Democrats will win appropriate by-elections, depriving Labour of the momentum it needs, stopping our bandwagon rolling and hence blocking our path to power.

Their impact at a general election depends on the prevailing forces of the time. After the Salad Wars, it may never be a glad, confident morning again for the third party. Yet if the long, slow rise in its voting has peaked (and there is no reason why it should have), the high level may well be maintained. They are in showbiz; an Action-Man routine is a good gimmick. All that will be lacking is the old illusion that they can displace Labour, which they so nearly pulled off in 1983 as they attempted to transfer by-election tactics to a general election. That conjuring trick may be more difficult, but hope springs eternal, particularly in foolish breasts, and this government just might generate more of the kind of vapid discontent that the third party feeds on.

Recovery between elections could be easy for the Democrats unless we move quickly to capture their ground, their images and their votes, and show ourselves to be the only alternative to Thatcherism, the only way of change and the party destined to win. We need a strategy for dealing with them for that is the game we now live or die by. They threaten us, not with a war to the death but with impotence. By deadlocking the system and leading a large section of the electorate into fantasy land, they entrench the government. Instead of forcing the Democrats to continue with that, we should use them as a stepping stone to a power that is unlikely now to be ours alone but could be ours mainly. Part of the coalition for change with which we won in the 1960s and now need to build again is with them, on terms that vary from full enlistment through general sympathy to protest reflex. We could, once, have gathered them all under our umbrella. We should still try but we may also have to work directly with the Democrats. Humpty Dumpty cannot be put back together, but he could be sat back on the wall, with help.

Looking at Britain's party balance, Continentals would say that it is workable only with PR, allowing under-parties to form coalitions, minorities to come to power, and sectional parties to build a national base. In PR, relationships would develop naturally. Without it, delusions are kept alive at the expense of realism. Consider, therefore, the lessons of competitive marketing. Just as every small car, soap powder and supermarket chain has to be much the same as the competition, so party competition now requires us to become more like the Democrats, to embrace their base, their issues and constituency, the better to displace them by using our market power to swamp their ground and drive them to the periphery. Party ideology pulls the other way: emphasize the differences, stand on separate ground. That has been fatal already for it has cleared the centre ground for them to occupy. Real competition requires us to be the same but better, nicer and certainly much better value because we have that added extra: the ability to take power and deliver. Indeed, we are the only party which can turn desire into reality.

This is not an argument for abandoning what we are in order to embrace their policies. To become the Democrats would be to give up our own market share, our brand image and our loyalties. We must, rather, add Liberalism to what we have by filching that substantial proportion of their clothes that fits and suits us, to widen our appeal. We do not abandon what we were because parties must cover the whole market range: not just the basic models (in this case, the issues) we are good at, such as caring and sharing (our Mini), but also the middle-range issues of individualism and success and the emerging civic issue that the Democrats have marketed so successfully to their middle-class constituency, as well as the top of the range (Jaguar) issues of quality, competence, ability and image that ensure that we will deliver. Embracing the Democratic base is not incompatible with socialism but enhances it. Liberalism and individualism cannot work without greater equality. Yet greater equality cannot now be sold without the liberal and individualistic trappings that appeal to a more pluralistic electorate.

So we move to the centre, drop extremism, soften hard edges and embrace the 'second order' issues that the Liberals have attempted to make their own but which they betray as they espouse because they can never implement them. Issues of citizenship and individualism are wholly appropriate to Labour. Having been brought so far by state support and collective provision, our new middle (*née* working) class demands empowerment – to be listened to, to have influence and not be ignored – a demand that can be fulfilled by rights as citizens, as workers, as consumers of services (particularly monopoly ones), by decentralization, by freedom of information, in itself a form of power. Britain's centralized, secretive state restricts democracy to a four-yearly choice between parties, a degree of involvement hardly appropriate to, or adequate for, a pluralistic, complex society and a better-educated electorate. The strong state has failed. The system with the greatest power and potential has delivered comparative failure, produced only alienation and frustration. Why not, therefore, develop a political strategy that corrects these failings and makes a virtue of something inevitable by dismantling the centralized machinery to the maximum possible degree, and passing its power out to the people?

The machinery of the British state is no longer something to be proud of. The people do not feel free but frustrated, not involved but alienated. The system is seen as cumbersome, outdated, authoritarian, Parliament as a fun factory fit only for Punch & Judy politics. Mrs Thatcher's authoritarian tantrums have endeared neither her nor a system that concentrates total power in her. Government-by-whim has discredited the structure. Labour will not now need the strong state to build socialism. We can do that by cooperation and management of the market. Why, therefore, keep it? Break it down, parcel it out to the people at political profit to ourselves and the gain of a genuinely new image as the party of freedom and democracy.

Proportional representation – representing the people's wish in Parliament – should be the central part of a wider process: entrenching rights, in the constitution, at work, to services, as citizens; decentralization of power by breaking down the dominance of the Great Wen and establishing regional governments, not only in Scotland and Wales but in all the English regions with powers transferred down from the centre and up from the counties (which should go). One-tier local government, based on the boroughs and districts with genuine powers and more independence, will then repair the damage done to the whole structure by Mrs Thatcher.

The party of freedom has allowed itself to be associated with despotism, alien monoliths, unions and block votes. If Labour embraces empowerment, it can undercut the appeal of the Democrats and build support among all to whom new issues are becoming more important than the old bread-and-butter ones that have been basic for so long. This is a revolutionary programme that should be natural for Labour. Having taken its people so far, it wants, as they do, to see them stand on their own two feet, facing the world and deciding their own destinies, self-confidently, not nervously and diffidently.

Young people are more independent-minded than their elders but still too diffident, for the fading class society still leaves them too conditioned to knowing their place, even if that place has changed. They lack the natural self-confidence of Americans and Australians. They are only part free. Labour has to help them the rest of the way, by empowering and emancipating, building a platform to freedom so they can walk in the world with the natural self-confidence of those born free.

Market competition and the dynamics of the party system both push Labour towards such a programme, but because political parties are less ready than companies to listen to market research, the alternatives must be put dramatically. We either beat the Democrats or we join them. Beating is not really possible and means wasting the efforts of both, hands in fraternal greeting round each other's throats, a spectacle the public loathes. Joining is not merger but marginalization – theirs. However many times Jeremy Thorpe, David Steel and now Paddy Ashdown tell their party to 'prepare for power', the Democrats are peddlers of dreams that can never happen, a cargo cult deceiving the people by offering escapism as a serious alternative. They cultivate the margins of the big field, and can play the grown-up power game only if Labour splits or dies. Labour and the Democrats must live together, if only because fighting strengthens the Dictatorene. So offer them gains in their margin game to make it worthwhile, in return for gains for us in the big league. The only loss is the abandonment of a majoritarianism that we can no longer sustain and fantasies that frustrate the realists.

The first stage is the establishment of working relationships. In the localities, these can be encouraged by abandoning Labour's sulky refusal to work three-party politics or come to arrangements with Democrats. They are devious. Their minority mentality, nurtured during the long years of opposition and impracticality, leads them to try to get the best of all worlds: mended pavements and reduced rates; Euro-enthusiasm but exploitation of every anti-market grumble. Parties – even our own – can only be weaned from such juvenilia by dealing with the problems and dilemmas of power. As Democrats face these, their choices on employment, education, services and social and economic issues generally will not be much different from those of realistic Labour politicians. Working together against the Tories, therefore, keeps that enemy out, protects local government and develops habits of contact, consultation and relationship at grass roots – as well as educating.

At the centre, Democrat MPs will hesitate to work with Labour for fear of being engulfed. This is, in fact, the aim, so their fears should not inhibit our approach. Open up contacts, establish consultation through whips and leaders, and sympathetic contacts between back benchers, all leading eventually to subject-by-subject consultation to coordinate responses to government actions. Amendments and motions should not aim at Labour goals exclusively but could be softened and broadened, to make refusal of Democrat support appear churlish. All this can be done with no great or real loss. Parties spend far too much time drawing fine lines that are invisible, incomprehensible or irrelevant to the electorate. Many people view Labour and the Democrats as interchangeable to some degree and they are certainly baffled by our failure to work together to stop Mrs Thatcher. The aim should be for anyone who wishes to take dissenting ground to be forced into marginalization, extremism or plain silliness. Proper tactics involve putting others into those irrelevant dustbins, rather than rushing to sit in them ourselves.

The ulterior motive behind such efforts should be an electoral arrangement. Both parties are against it – an instinctive, negative reaction springing from party prejudice, not practical calculation. It puts petty – and, in fact, misunderstood – party interests higher than those of, either the nation or the party as a whole. An arrangement reached before the election could make a difference of 20 to 40 seats to the Tory party. When the government will be losing seats but not probably enough, that could make all the difference.

Anyone who sees the best interests of Britain in a Tory defeat must consider a pact. So should realistic Labour people who prefer power to polishing the purity of their principles in opposition, as well as Democrats who prefer a useful role and some share of power to being right all the time, a privilege accorded only to the impotent. If these three groups do not together constitute a majority of the forces immobilized outside the narrow Tory camp, Britain deserves the Conservative government it will undoubtedly keep. If they cannot organize themselves for sense, they too deserve the castration that they will undoubtedly suffer.

Yet if the groups can come together, they tap new reserves of support from a public that wishes such a consummation. Labour can show itself as accommodating, realistic and moderate, as it needs to be. The Democrats can make some contact with reality. Both parties should openly and seriously discuss it, not ban even talk of it as if the mere consideration of the possibility of defeat were treason. Arguing for an arrangement is not abandoning the fight for a Labour majority. That must continue with every resource and sinew. It is the *summum bonum*: what both party and nation really need. However, partisanship so great that it eclipses all reason is futile, and because Labour has slid so far back while this government has entrenched itself, there is a mountain to climb. Therefore, a Labour majority is the goal that should be worked for as singlemindedly and determinedly as if all depends on it, which it does. But take out insurance. An arrangement improves the odds, reduces the risks and does more damage to the enemy at the cost of a sacrifice only of hopes which are as illusory as the consequences of failure are harsh.

An elaborate, full-scale deal that divides the country and allocates seats to parties as the Mis-Alliance did in its imperial phase is not part of the argument. Parties must approach relationships as cautiously as porcupines make love. They invariably affront local activists everywhere so the aim should be limited to persuading those who have no prospect that their sacrifice for the greater good will help the party and can ultimately strengthen their own position. Even more limited proposals can build on developments on the ground that are already going on, and which will work for both parties – just as Herbert Gladstone and Ramsey MacDonald built the first Lib–Lab electoral arrangement of 1905 on what was actually happening in the double-member boroughs. The electorate has already begun to vote tactically – in unwinable Tory seats and in the seats for which Labour has huge majorities (the 28 biggest majorities are all Labour). There, the Labour vote has fallen away, though it has kept up in marginals where every vote counts. Tactical voting has also begun to be seen as a means of changing incumbents in neighbouring seats. Take the 1987 contrast between the two Oxford seats. In East Oxford, Labour won narrowly, with 43 per cent of the vote, compared to 16 per cent for the Alliance. In South Oxford, Labour came third with 15 per cent, the Tories holding the seat with a majority of 7 per cent over the Alliance, which had 37 per cent of the vote. Electors had made two very different but equally realistic calculations in the neighbouring seats, so that opposition support in each went to the best-placed opposition candidate.

That may be a one-off, an indication that an educated Southern electorate is capable of deciding its own priorities, yet such pairings have also been seen in less elegant regions such as Yorkshire. In the neighbouring seats of Ryedale (Labour 8 per cent, Alliance 39 per cent) and York (Labour 41 per cent, Alliance 16 per cent), exactly the same thing happened but attracted less attention because Labour just failed to win the York seat while the Alliance lost its earlier by-election gain in Ryedale. York may not be an ideal example because it is a university town, so take rougher Shipley (Labour 23 per cent, Alliance 26 per cent) and neighbouring Keighley (Labour 35 per cent, Alliance 19 per cent), or Pudsey (Labour 20 per cent, Alliance 34 per cent) and nearby Batley (Labour 41 per cent, Alliance 14 per cent).

Half-a-dozen such pairs can be readily identified. In all of them, electors are doing, to greater or lesser degree, what the parties fear to do on an organized basis. Power is slipping from the parties. That loss of control will go further next time. In the last election, the trend was more marked in the North, Scotland and Wales, where the electoral tide ran against the government, than in the South, where it ran to it. When the national trend runs against a tired Tory government, all electors will have a motive to calculate how to achieve an aim that will then be more widely shared. Another campaign for tactical voting will emerge to give direction to that wish. It will probably be more effective than last time, and sufficient to affect seats, rather than just votes, because it will then be with a stronger tide. Labour and the Democrats could sulk and hope that the electorate's wish to get the government out will help one of them rather than the other. They would be more usefully employed boosting the tide. That requires a national arrangement, including local pairings in a broader deal that will offer the Democrats gains in the South-west where it is strong and Labour gains in the North-west and the West Midlands where it is dominant and there is no chance of a Democrat breakthrough.

The number of seats to be covered is a matter of precise calculation and detailed negotiation. No more than 100 is necessary; less would do. The deal must offer something to both parties. Labour fears that it offers all to the Democrats, that they would be given a boost into becoming a real force. But that would be the electorate's decision. Labour would lose its claim that it is going to win on its own. That is not going to happen anyway, and reptiles have to adjust to reality, not try to play dinosaurs and pretend that they still rule the world. Chameleons have survived by constantly changing colour.

Labour would lose support only in seats it cannot win, where its vote is low and getting lower. Yet it feels, with more justice, that although it can deliver such votes to Democrats, the latter cannot do the same in return because their vote, being basically a protest, is drawn from 'soft Conservatives' who might not be able to face the social trauma of voting Labour. This fear is boosted by another: that of giving the Democrats firm roots. The best reason why such fears are irrelevant is that the Democrats worry about much the same thing. In their wilder moments of surging support, they develop majoritarian delusions, that Labour is in terminal decline. They too fear to alienate the support they have built up. More Liberal MPs have won seats by attracting the Tory vote than by eating into Labour's, and they will feel threatened. Democrats also see the Labour vote as already being more squeezed in those seats from which Labour candidates would withdraw than is the Alliance vote in seats from which Democrats would withdraw.

Yet the main support for these views comes from the area of most intense conflict: local government. Here, Labour has already authorized pacts for local purposes. In any case, realistic assessment casts a cold eye on both sets of fears. The Labour vote is more deliverable, but the problem is to stop it deserting altogether when Democrats are second and alone able to turn out the Tories. The Democrats are more difficult. Many Alliance voters were protest voters, more anti-socialist than anti-Tory, and as a result, the Lib–Lab pact probably lost the Liberals support in the 1979 election. Yet losses and the fate of the vote both depend on the mood of the time. The bigger the anti-Tory swing, the greater the prospect of either side delivering its voters to the other. The greatest help that Mrs Thatcher could give would be to stay on as Tory leader.

With no liberal candidate, the Liberal/Alliance/Democrat vote has split 50:50 between Labour and Tories. With the Tories in power, the Democrats have become more identified against them, inclining their vote more towards Labour. With persuasion, they might fall 60:40 to Labour, a transfer of one-fifth of their vote. Calculate four-fifths as the similar proportion for Labour voters who would go to the Democrats, apply both rates to as many as necessary, and when the third-placed withdraws to the benefit of the second, the result would be 32 Labour gains, 29 Democrat. Such a rough equality arises because, while the Labour vote is more deliverable, it is much smaller in those seats that are Tory/Democrat marginals than the Democrat vote is in Tory/Labour marginals.

Opponents heighten fear by claiming that pacts will apply to all seats and now. In fact, a range of options and times is available. Sense suggests late arrangements with each section of the opposition striving for supremacy in the long run-up and doing deals only as it becomes clear that neither can win. Labour could pledge a referendum on PR to attract Democrat votes without any mention of an electoral arrangement. Yet it would be wiser to look to mutual withdrawals in 30 seats each, leaving the party fight to go on in the rest. Labour could best help the Democrats by withdrawing their top 30 marginals. We must assume that we will win those seats ranging from York to Slough that will fall to a 4 per cent swing on our own efforts. If we can't, we may as well give up. So if the Democrats withdraw in the next 30 marginals most would be vulnerable to a 4 per cent swing, coupled with a fifth of the old Alliance vote, putting Labour in sight of government. On this basis it is possible to develop a deal in the light of public opinion as the election approaches, one that would bring a loss to the Tories great enough to deprive them of office – on a 4 per cent swing against the government, as opposed to the 6 per cent necessary without such a deal. This would restore to Labour the extra edge it lost in 1987. It would also be largely free of the odium that might attach to a deal involving all seats, for each party would be fighting largely on its own but each would be seeking to maximize the result for the other. We would be asking the electorate to vote mostly Labour or Democrat, but giving them the extra bonus of getting the government out.

Objections come from those on the Labour side in hopeless areas that contribute nothing to the party's prospects locally or nationally, and from Democrats for whom hopes of miracles, the party's fig leaf, outweigh practical sense. These groups, and leaderships whose prestige is involved, see pacts as confessions of failures. So they are, but they could also be described as an admission of reality. The fact is that neither party can achieve anything separately, and accepting practicalities opens up possibilities. Purity closes bedroom doors.

This hints at a sexual problem for, as with relationships, one thing leads to another. An electoral arrangement will benefit the people by giving them the lever to turn out this government. They will, however, want to know the colour of the horse, and the Tory pulverizing machine will be turned loose to unpick and discredit any arrangement that threatens them. So the deal must be sewn up in other areas, too. Specifically, this would mean the governmental arrangements, proportional representation, which will be a *sine qua non* for the Democrats, and an agreed, minimum programme – in other words, the common agenda. The arrangements and the programme depend on the circumstances of the time and the balance of the negotiations and will, in any case, only be reached as the election approaches.

Full coalition would dismay the ranks of both parties and is not on the cards, though the possibility could always be aired, just to help them to see that the actual arrangement is a lesser evil. There is, however, a growing demand for such agenda and a broad alternative. It is up to the parties to satisfy that, emphasizing for public consumption that such an arrangement puts power in their hands since the nature of the new government and the balance of its programme will both be finally decided by the electorate. Labour, as the greater part of the governing majority, will dominate, but an understanding on the nature of Democrat support and participation, particularly in respect of matters of confidence and the basics of the programme,will give the incoming government a guarantee and the electorate an alternative (as distinct from a Thatcher exterminator). It will also be in line with overseas practice. In West Germany, coalition partners announce their betrothal beforehand. In Sweden, the bourgeois parties provide a minimum joint agenda and retain separate positions on the rest. Something similar will be essential here.

Negotiations must cover electoral reform, not by requiring Labour to swallow whole what only the farsighted have so far nibbled at, but undertaking to submit PR to a referendum within the life of the Parliament, with the government remaining benignly neutral and Labour MPs allowed to campaign in favour, or against if any are so foolhardy as to undermine the base on which their new government will rest, and which will bind the Democrats to it. The referendum could not, of course, be held in the first year and could, with profit, be postponed for longer, though it should occur before any defining election is called to clarify the electoral situation. The prospects of carrying PR in the referendum depend on the success of the government itself, just as the prospects of devolution depended on this in 1979. The electorate is favourable in general terms but doubtful in specifics, so the best augury for success would be the demonstration by a successful government that the new politics work and that an electoral arrangement delivers.

There can be no greater inducement for the two main elements of anti-Tory opinion to work together and ensure that a government of national unity succeeds. Each would be under pressure to make the referendum a success as well as the government. The new politics and a new electoral system would provide the only prospect of success for either. In recognizing this, they would be fulfilling the wishes of the electorate and building a more democratic system. No Democrat, Social or Liberal, who wants electoral reform is serious unless they envisage cooperation with Labour to get it. No one in the Labour Party who wants power is realistic unless they envisage electoral reform as part of the process. Both are obscurantist unless they recognize their need for each other.

The traditionalists – a.k.a. the Left – will decline to consider such a scheme. The cautious, conformist Right of the Labour Party will be doubtful about any approximation to the Democrats for, as the group that has the most in common with similar 'sound' chaps in other parties, they must differentiate themselves the more frantically by posing as 'soft left'. They will not endanger that exercise by the realism that durst not speak its name. As the Labour Party's prospects improve and its poll ratings go up, the reasons for not speaking it will become ever stronger. Anyone who does will be denounced as rocking a boat heading for harbour – but not reaching it. Labour is too strong to do deals, too weak to win without them. So a choice that would be difficult for a realistic political party may be impossible for Labour. Yet gambling is no way to build socialism, and Labour plays a casino: its number may come up, but more likely it will not. That still leaves another turn later, but as it waits, its prospects recede: through redistribution; because its Scottish base is threatened; and because the people and interests it defends are set further back. The possibility of doing anything recedes. The country goes downhill.

Labour can win in 1991. More people are up for grabs so the potential for change is greater. A government driven by one will, particularly one as active and unbalanced as this, could generate a massive reaction, even fall apart, like the one horse shay or Boadicea's chariot. It is now moving to the wilder shores of Thatcherism yet neither a cabinet of subordinates nor a party that actually believes in her dare take the Ayatollahrine by the arm to murmur 'enough is enough'. Just as the path to promotion in the Labour Party is by disloyalty to the left, in the Tories it is via servility. As a result, Labour's weakness is that it cannot be led, the Conservatives' that they can be led too far.

With the underpinning of prosperity removed, the government has begun its long downhill ride. It couldn't have happened to a nicer crowd. The weatherhouse of politics is already causing the government to retreat and bringing the opposition to the fore, changing the mood so that what looked impossible and impractical one year will take on a whole new attractive power the next. It all resembles the scrapbook for 1959–64, and the process could again lead to victory for Labour. Yet all are possibilities, not yet proven facts, and the odds are against such staples working in the old way.

Labour's prospects of outright victory in 1991 are slight but will become substantially less if we do not change than if we do. An effort to change by broadening the party, embracing new policies and coming to deals with the rest of the opposition will not necessarily produce success, but it is the only programme that offers any prospect, and most of it will have to be done anyway, at some stage. Better, therefore, to embark on it early to boost the prospect of getting the Conservatives out in 1991. Later, the situation will be far more desperate, decline less reversible, talent will have been drained away from the opposition, hope from the nation, and people will be looking for the man on the white horse, not cooperation, altruism and brotherhood. Bloody heads drain bleeding hearts. Labour is the party of democratic socialism or it is nothing, and it is not in its interest to wait for ever in the hope of power and a majority on its terms, but to fulfil its historic destiny of saving the nation. Power in 1991 is opportunity to rebuild and to get the credit for repairing the damage done by Thatcherism. Power in 1996 is a very different – and still far from certain – proposition.

Unless the Labour Party understands its situation, it will not attempt the massive changes necessary to operate successfully in a new political environment. It must become a broad movement for the majority, instead of a defensive movement for those left behind. It must marginalize the Democrats. Unless it does both, it relegates itself to its ghetto.

Having taken these two major steps, it is but a minor further one to give the whole process a real prospect of success by an electoral arrangement to turn out the government, with electoral reform as an essential part. This would attract new support and round off the process of liberalization within the Labour Party. It would also open up the way to the coalition politics of cooperation appropriate to an advanced pluralistic society. This is not new to Britain – the parties themselves are coalitions, though on both sides the recent pressure has been to make them less representative of the wider society – and it is normal elsewhere. Labour should now widen its grasp by working with other parties.

Taking power, succeeding and thus showing that Labour can deliver are the only ways back to being a natural party of government. The prospect of governing on its own, as the SPO has done in Austria's PR system and the SAP in Sweden's, is the ultimate goal, but present reality is coalition politics or at the very least party cooperation. We must learn to walk before we attempt running.

The aims of Labour and the Democrats broadly overlap. Indeed, as Labour moved to the centre of the road and dropped EC withdrawal and unilateralism, there has been a broad covergence heightened by Labour's belated efforts to catch up on constitutional positions. Socialism is distinct from Liberalism, but we are decades from such ultimates, and each is incomplete without the other. So why not march as far as we can together, allowing Labour to stop the counter-revolution and to govern, making the Democrats practical instead of acting as a collection of eccentric individualists masquerading as a party. Facing the real world might diminish their appeal, but they must decide what game they want to play: fantasy fun or the power game.

Both parties owe it to Britain. Society should be allowed to adjust and the people to have their wishes turned into policy. The people should be involved in the system and given a stake in government and Parliament. Their votes will say what they want. If that is Margaret Thatcher, so be it (and God help the rest). If, as is more likely, they want better policies from two parties neither of whom they trust on their own, those parties must work together. That is the will of the people, and parties exist to implement it, not to sulk or impose their own prejudices. That leads only to frustration and alienation.

Labour is obsessed with the romance of socialism. That is mainly, now, our own escapism. It should be obsessed with reality: the people, what they want and how to give it to them. Coalition politics are the name of that game. Most advanced societies have it because they are more complex and pluralistic. Britain has become both, as the class monoliths have broken down. As a result, coalition politics are struggling to be born, trying to break out of the constraints of a rigid, atrophying electoral and party system that asks a complex society to fit into two buckets, and restricts democracy to a five-yearly choice between alternatives people do not particularly like. That hardly satisfies the diverse, contradictory wishes of a pluralistic society. It must go so that the new non-party politics that have been struggling to be born since the 1960s can finally emerge. It cannot do this in a third-party role, for that position dooms it and everything planted there. The third party is a symptom not a cure. It strengthens the antithesis of freedom: Thatcherism.

Yet by standing left of centre, the home of causes, always quirky, idealistic, naïve and difficult to fit into the tight constraints of party, the effort to build the new politics becomes viable. It also turns that sector of politics from failed party into dynamic mass cause to counter the one dominant party. As a middle-ground phenomenon (different from a third-party phenomenon), it can articulate the aspirations of both the moderate majority and the liberal cause peddlers who have both been steamrollered by ten years of party-rule-turned dictatorship. Both can find a useful role if they cooperate in people-friendly politics to eliminate the dictatorship of the will by spreading power and making the system sensitive to the wishes of the people. A political system that involves the people and listens to them is more appropriate to the sophisticated, educated, pluralistic electorate of an advanced industrial nation than the class-divided politics of a faded imperial power, led by an élite that has failed.

10

Beyond the Blue Horizon Lies a Rising Sun?

Great leaders rise to the times. In Britain, the times shrank to Margaret Thatcher. Brought to office by a series of accidents and kept there by Labour follies, she has used her decade to carry out a counter-revolution, not to tackle the economic problems that gave her her chance in the first place. No real success, no cataclysmic failure, just ten years marching down a dead-end street, wasting the oil opportunity, leaving Britain to stagnate. Her government went from excessive stringency through foolish irresponsibility back to stringency, a triumph of public relations and unbalanced activity but a waste of time for everything else. The last opportunity is the one that cannot be missed, yet after a decade of oil, the British economy can neither support the standard of living nor provide the growth that a consumer society needs. It cannot pay Britain's way or provide jobs for between 2.6 and 3.4 million of its people, though the government no longer wants to know the true figure because it is no longer any guide to policy. They have abandoned social responsibility for the million long-term un-employed and the huge, new sub-class of 9 million 'new poor', up by one — third in ten years. All are ever further distanced from the pawky well-being of the semi-affluent. Tax cuts for the rich, thin gruel and thick lectures for the bottom half have meant a massive shift in social balances, compounded by the rise in unemployment, producing a harder, meaner society. The whittling away of community and state has meant that anyone who is dependent would suffer quite disproportion-ately in a society that demanded that you 'stand on your own two feet' when too many could not. In the 1930s, the poor were the broad base of the pyramid, a common human lot — not, as they are now, a species of privatized leper, forced to take their misery home and close the door.

After a decade of Mother Maggie's Remedy, Britain has all the outward and visible signs of a failing society; poverty, unemployment, homelessness, crime, the prison population, all at record or near record levels; drug addiction, up five-fold; sales of champagne doubled. It is still a class society, but one with no class any more. A creaking, crumbling, shabby failure, the first nation to turn 'under repair' into a way of life. Traffic grinds to a halt on badly maintained, over-stressed roads and motorways. Railways and tubes are overcrowded, late, breaking down. London and the South-east choke up. The consequences of years of neglect and cost-cutting come through in disasters – King's Cross, Clapham Common, the *Herald of Free Enterprise*, salmonella poisoning – holding out for the Prime Minister a full-time future indulging her macabre passion to play Nightingale to the nation by visiting the victims of her own failure to invest, or, in the case of food, inspect.

The shoddiness of Britain's manufactured goods in the 1960s has been transferred to the public sector, and not only because we have ceased to make the goods. Private affluence/public squalor is the reality, its encapsulating image a crawling motorway narrowed to one lane, the rest closed for repairs that never seem to happen, the drivers of the jammed BMWs and Mercs using Japanese Yodelphones to call wives stuck in bijou, British-built boxes, doodling on the in-car fax, or listening to imported CDs on imported audio systems, built into the boot lest they be stolen by the natives.

Britain offers the world nothing and goes nowhere. Its pensioner welfare state is shabby, its standards and services below those of richer competitors. The premier products and well-known marques that it once sold round the world are gone, or a guise for imports. To lead in nothing is to be vulnerable in everything. The great adventures of commerce and industry have run down and out, into the fiddler's short-changing calculus, the scrap merchant's quick speculative profit. The first industrial society has become a financial casino, twisted by knaves to make a trap for fools.

What remains of greatness? Industrial or technological, research or educational supremacies? Superior institutions or dignified traditions of public service? Industrial might? All gone. Only the Arthur Daley economy of ramps, lurks, fiddles, takeovers and market manipulation, as a nation on the make tries to make it without bothering with the tawdry business of training, investing, researching, developing or following the pedestrian paths of West Germans, Japanese, Koreans or lesser breeds without the City. Britain is in danger of becoming a scrounger nation: America's fag and the world's scavenger, arms salesman, money manipulator, mercenary and general dirty dealer.

The end of oil's best years offers little hope of improving on that. Britain's problems are too serious to be hit with a handbag or dealt with at the intellectual level of 'Disgusted of Grantham', but this government has no alternative. Deflation will bite deep. With the ever-present possibility of a world slump as a background, Houdini gimmickry has degenerated into a race between the intended fall in house prices to burst the bubble and the possible collapse of confidence in sterling, to which we are more exposed than ever before. The first may reduce interest rates (eventually), the second will increase them but, in the meantime, there is stagflation: another government back in the old British trap but unable to admit it because it cannot learn and will not change. A failed government that has run out of answers must first be dug out to stop decline while there is still chance.

Labour hopes, against hope, for another 1945: a new dawn of social reconstruction. Britain needs a New Deal to build a strong economy. Both are noble visions and inspirations for patriots who crave something better for their benighted country. Yet both are impossible for each requires a change of government. The Soviet Union's one-party dictatorship can change. Britain's elective dictatorship cannot.

There are enough conventional reasons why it will be difficult to defeat this government: Labour is doing all that party wisdom suggests, but its bandwagon moves only slowly, always in danger of being eclipsed by the Democrats' flash-wagon. The government is cunning, well able to manipulate opinion, a pliant media and the economy, and ready to use the election support fund it has given itself in budget surpluses of £20 to £30 billion each year ahead that have built up because it will not spend. Although this has been the worst government of recent decades, the book of the next election is not yet written.

Britain's party system no longer works in the old way. The two-party system rested on a two-class society. As that fades, parties must forge new coalitions, and as conditioning weakens, they must sell to the uncommitted. The Conservatives did this by reaching out with their populist message to the Cs, Ds and even Es. Meanwhile Labour busily alienated its Cs, Bs and As by its intolerance and incompetence, compounding its problems as the Tories countered theirs.

Belatedly finding that mass parties wither in an age of mass leisure and non-party politics, Labour tried to stitch together a patchwork coalition of minorities, which turned out to be more Bertram Mills than Jesse Jackson. It found that multiplication of demands divides support. The later, more sensible strategy has been to rebuild the conventional party, with wider membership and blander policies, but doing this in an age of anti-party politics. The Prime Minister has discovered the benefits of being non-political, even running against politics and her own party and government. The media focus on personality creation, which Labour, as a party of restricted charisma growth and in opposition, finds it difficult to adjust to. The hope was that, if the alternative was restored, the leverage of the two-party system would work and a blandwagon would ride to power. It may, given a dramatic increase in volatility and a Thatcher government opting for a hitherto well-concealed preference for political suicide.

Margaret Thatcher believes government should be as 'hands on' as the Venus de Milo, but her own practice is to be more like the Goddess Kali or a kleptomaniac octopus. The intervention by impulse that this gives rise to, on every issue from the ozone layer to trains through Kent, risks both explosive resentment and prime ministerial folly. Yet such short-term opportunism can also wrongfoot the opposition. Labour is dedicated, serious and as doubtful about opportunism and populism as a coachload of *Guardian* editors invited to a massage parlour: making excuses before entry. To every hope there is a despair. The 'Ourselves Alone' approach puts Labour at the mercy of entrenched incumbents and assumes that past masters will unlearn the lessons of power.

What is needed is clearheaded, strategic thinking. The Tories are single-minded about power. Labour is woolly-headed and would rather not air differences by thinking through its priorities. This is why it failed in the 1960s: those who stand for nothing achieve it and serving the people then took third place to being clever and staying in power. This is also why, after 1979, the party opted for strategies that made power less likely and Labour even less able to handle it than it had been before. In our situation we cannot afford illusions. We must think everything through and be absolutely clear about our priorities. The first, second and third is the people: not ideology; not posing for the party, nor making it an instrument for socialism, but making the people better off. To do that, we need power. To get that, we must add new groups to the hard core to which folly has reduced us, broadening and diluting our appeal to win support generally, and aiming particularly at the middle-class groups we have lost to the Democrats, and at the groups lower down, particularly the skilled workers, many of whom were lured to the Tories by the prospect of cash-in-hand gains for themselves.

The former need liberal policies and expect us to pay off the humanity deficit of this government with a great education and re-education programme. The latter prefer the decent, human face of populism, which offers concrete practical prospects of economic growth, jobs and a great reskilling. To attract both groups requires us to move away from the old working-class, trade union party to become a classless coalition for change: a broad movement for betterment that offers hope and movement, optimism and prospects, rather than duty and discipline. Not strengthening the party mould as we now intend, but breaking it. Less of a party, more a rally for progress.

A major swing against the government is building up, demonstrated by record falls in the Tory vote at by-elections: Richmond's was even bigger than Orpington's. Because of the distribution of Labour's vote and support, this does not now offer us the prospect of being the largest single party by default. This happened in 1974, and even then it would not have without Harold Wilson's advantage of having a dissolution in his back pocket conceded because of Heath's unconsummated flirtation with Jeremy Thorpe. Today, the third party is stronger, and we are weaker. So the change now in progress could be like an arctic spring: lavish colour flowering in the tundra, an air of renewal that the mood projection machine of the media will build up as if Labour were actually in power, only to prick their own bubble as they get tired of it. Below the surface phenomena, the electoral ground is still deep frozen.

Salutory change has begun. The party is edging towards much of what needs to be done. Once reselection is over and MPs can put their heads above the parapet more will advocate deals. Yet what is lacking is any sense of the scale of the problem or the enormity of what must be done. The size of this government's majority and Labour's preventive detention in the peripheries make exceptional measures necessary. That means dealing with the Democrats – preferably both Liberal and Social, but certainly the former – to maximize the electoral damage to the government. Rebuilding the broad coalition of 1945 or 1964–6 within the one party must be pursued, as must every party strategy of 'Ourselves Alone' politics. Yet all may now be impossible without a deal to bring sections of the old army now enrolled elsewhere back into real politics by mobilizing them for the central national purpose. That means a working relationship through their new parties, the better to defeat a government that stands in the way of progress, the nation, the future.

Some envisage deals after the 1991 election. That will be too late. They must come first to destroy this government's majority. That done, the vacuum has to be filled. There is now no way of doing that which can give us, as socialists, all we want, or deliver an exclusively Labour government. The hopes for a government with power to destroy the bases of the class system by tackling wealth and delivering equality through the massive redistribution that Britain needs and the war on poverty that it deserves are but dreams. As for coming out of the European Community, cutting the defence burden massively, getting rid of nuclear weapons or taking back what belongs to all of us but has been sold to give tax cuts to some, all such policies are as desirable as they are unlikely. Labour will not ask for and would not get a majority for any of them.

The best becomes the enemy of the good, and radicalism becomes alien to a party busily smoothing its every edge.

If Labour can do little on its own, a stronger government can be built on the spirit of cooperation to bring down the Tories. It can throw Thatcherism into reverse and start out on the road to the fair society. There is enough common ground between Labour, Social and Liberal Democrats to offer a limited, consensus programme, based on a self-denying ordnance from Labour and realism from the third party or parties. This would give Democrats some, us more, and the people all they want, a distinct improvement on the forced diet of Thatcherism. Such a government would also be people-friendly. The nation wants parties to work together for the common purpose rather than bicker and fight, each asserting its primacy when none has any.

We would, therefore, work for a Labour government with a majority to govern, but we would have to recognize that, if that is not available, Britain can still have a broad-bottom government that offers hope and provides Labour with a platform to build on. The electoral arrangement with the Democrats should envisage a consensus government and its programme, for when people vote out a government, they want to know what will replace it, being less likely to do so if they do not. What is feasible is all that is necessary. The common agenda should cover the major Liberal–Democrat contribution – a broad programme of political and constitutional reform, of the type that is now being espoused by Labour – and the Labour requirement of repair to the damaged structures of industry and industrial relations, welfare, health and social security. The environmental and 'lifestyle' strategy, attempting a new settlement between society and the physical world, would be common to both parties, as would the shifting of the social balances between markets and community. *Pace* monetarist mythology: there are no perfect markets, just as the latter are right in saying that there is no perfect government. What is needed is not total reversal but a new settlement: more state, less market in the environment, health and education, but not excluding either when they serve the paramount purposes of the people rather than ideology. The economic strategy could also be in common; Labour and Democrats have both accepted the fundamentals of economic expansion based on incomes policy, cheap money, regional support, proper training, a competitive currency, running the economy for people and jobs, not money, managing markets, not abdicating to them, cooperating not controlling. Here are the essentials of success; a programme that eschews extremes and *dirigeste* methods and uses the market to regenerate the natural dynamics of the economy. It builds on the common ground towards which all the opposition parties have been moving, Labour most vigorously of all. It also happens to be the programme that the people want.

The further catalogue of policies that party supporters want are now sectional demands not the main menu. They can only be achieved if they fall off the back of a mandate. The electorate is tired of parties, their bickering, their failures and the interminable games that fascinate them but bore everyone else. It wants change, a sense of purpose and hope, an alternative that expresses the wishes of the nation, not the quirks of a minority. It can get all this if the opposition parties each give up something and work together on the public agenda. By abandoning the unattainable, they, and Britain, get most of what is necessary, and an opening to bring in other policies later, provided they deliver on the essentials first. Socialists will continue to work for the better society but actual movement towards it will replace the constant frustration of trying to convince a free-market steamroller driver of the error of her ways. Democrats will apply themselves to the real world, instead of trying for the best of all worlds. People will be put back into the picture. The people, Lord, the people. Not parties and prescriptions but men, and women. The nation will be brought together instead of being divided by the implacable will.

Labour's paramount need is to show that it can both govern, and deliver. Only office and success can do that. A government dominated by Labour, with broad humanitarian sympathies, implementing the public agenda and determined on cooperation rather than discipline, can repair the damage and put Britain on the road to success. Nothing would do more to redeem Labour, and this is probably the only way now that the job can be done. So prospects open up as the fruits come through. Public support, growing from success, will provide the credibility on which to build back to majority status again. Labour can save enough planks from the wreckage to build the platform it needs to reach a new life. People may not vote for it now, but with success they will vote to sustain it.

New prospects for the parties open up Britain's opportunity to break out of the political deadlock. They also allow the political system to adjust to the new society. That system is in uneasy transition from a failing two-party system to the emerging politics of pluralism. The people sense that what was has failed. They do not like what is but are bemused about it, and can neither agree on nor prescribe the alternatives, while the politicians who should lead them continue to play their party games, waiting to be told by people and polls what to do. Meanwhile the Prime Minister tests the supreme power that the political vacuum has given her to destruction and uses her freedom to tear off in every available wrong direction. The only escape from the trap is to combine the inchoate wish of the electorate for a more people-friendly politics with the needs of the opposition parties to break the Tory hegemony.

Giving the people what they want has not been the basis of our politics since the war. Government by Party precludes it. Two-party politics are sensitive because parties compete for popular support. Yet having won it, they hold the enormous powers of the elective dictatorship, so the actual policies become a blend of what party activists, constantly tugging to left and right, want, and what the people will accept. This makes for a messy process in which governments lurch between implementing programmes and a craven crawling back to Elastoplast remedies, while the people are asked not to choose between alternative policies but to react to what governments do and usually to the pain of failed policies, producing a reaction against the incumbent – any and every incumbent. The consequence of this balance between parties without clear differentiation and a public without power or ability to enforce its own vague wishes, was confusion, lack of continuity and failure of leadership. Government was too democratic to lead, too pressured to be firm. The results were economic failure and public alienation, the one heightening the other. Britain's institutions did not deliver the growth and well-being most other democratic systems give to their electorates. Other nations moved ahead fast. We got nowhere slowly, throwing away every advantage in the process as involvement, respect for democratic institutions, support for parties and the system all faded. These could only have been sustained had the system delivered.

The public's wishes were, and are, simple: to be better off; to have better prospects for themselves and their children; to have growth, peace and certainty. Instead they got crises, constraints, turmoil and destruction, changes which eliminated industries, neighbourhoods, institutions and jobs, and destabilized everything without producing the rewards of prosperity and industrial power that resulted from successful change in nations going somewhere. The people realized that all was not well but could not influence it by votes, most of which were wasted. Their response was a loss of faith in both parties and institutions, a growing support for the third party and increasingly negative politics.

They were protesting – in their way. The parties responded with all the flexibility of a tram. Instead of offering more power to the people, they opted for the blind forces of ideology: more extreme versions of their own truth: be better socialists or be more conservative and all would be well. They crawled into their shells, but far from reviving the party system, this hibernation tested it to destruction and led to a festival of extremism that heightened the previous reactions against parties and politics.

Yet those like Roy Jenkins who attempted to give leadership, form and political expression to the public aspirations for non-party, non-extremist, non-ideological 'people politics' made the mistake of egotistically hitching their wagon to third-party politics, which invalidated every aspiration, doomed every hope. A third party in a 'first-past-the-post' electoral system means cargo cultism as a political lifestyle. The mistake was not the mission but the chosen location for the new edifice. Middle ground was the right place but a third party was not the right base. There lies futility. If 'non-party', more people-friendly politics are to break down the rigidities of an atrophied party system, it can only be through the real leverage of a viable party – that must be Labour. Still strong enough to prevent any alternative emerging, but no longer powerful enough to win on its own, Labour needs the extra strength and the new approach that taking over the faltering attempt to change the system can bring. Mobilizing the reaction against a failed system to amplify and widen the normal reaction against a failed government can provide the boost Labour needs, and bring it into line with widespread public aspirations. Moving with the tide allows Labour to lead Britain out of the age of two-party politics into the politics of pluralism, people politics and the public agenda. The deadlock on which Margaret Thatcher has based her power as Ice Queen is broken and Britain's politics are free to adjust naturally to the complexities of a new society, conforming to the new landscape and its luxuriant growth, rather than crushing everything like an ice cap left behind by time.

These transitions can be effected via proportional representation, by giving people a real choice and coalition politics that take decisions out of the parties and put them between, giving the public more power to intervene and be heard, easing the unilateral grip of the parties via decentralization and by shifting power and decisions back to the people. Coincidentally these are now the strategies that offer Labour its best prospects of breaking out of its ghetto. Combining Labour's needs with the nation's can allow the dictatorship of the minority to be succeeded by the democracy of the majority, and permit the new politics to emerge. Less predictable, probably more infuriating, but certainly more democratic because the people will state what they want and the politicians will have to put it into effect, becoming servants not masters, while power will flow out between the parties. Once parties become agencies of the people and not machines of tyranny, they will have to give the people what they want, rather than imposing party wills on the people's preferences.

The alternative to a compromise between Her Majesty's multiple oppositions must be political deadlock and a resumption of decline, first comparative, then absolute. Cumulative economic processes will be compounded by peripheralization and increasing irrelevance. God who made us feeble, make us feebler yet. What else offers? To live on fat? Too much has been gobbled, too much investment scrimped. To coast along on existing skills, acquired intellectual capital, the supportive networks built up over the years? All are now under provided, over strained, but need to be serviced, developed and improved to stay relevant to a fast-changing world.

Nations in difficulties are advised to develop comparative advantage. Where is Britain's? Not proximity to markets, ease of transport, high skills or an educated population. Not even low labour costs, nor new industries and technologies, for development comes to a dynamic base. Not, now, excellence, when we have thrown research, design and development overboard to stay afloat, slashed training, and substituted makework, or state training. Our universities have been forced to cut back and lose their brightest and best to the United States, and our only real areas of excellence – pure research, science and élite education – have all been made meaner. Excellence is exiled, its practitioners forced abroad. The decline from first rate has already gone a long way towards relegation. We are third rate now. Fourth to come. The processes have taken their grip. Britain is well up the excretory creek, its only paddle interest rates – which will not work.

In the 1950s and '60s Britain lost out in world markets. In the 1970s and '80s, it lost its home market, much of it gone to imports. Manufacturing firms such as ICI have transferred weight overseas. 'British' names from Vauxhall and Ford through Amstrad as well as large sections of the electronics and textile industries are covers for imports. Cars showed the way. The decline of domestic production handed two-fifths of the market to Europe, over one-tenth to Japanese, and left firms such as Ford, GM and Peugeot able to source more and more of their domestic sales from overseas production. In 1974, 44 per cent of Ford's production was in the UK. By 1988, it had declined to 27 per cent but this constituted two-fifths of its profits, a milch cow producing a profit flow to be invested in modern new plants in Europe so that the company could eventually shift production there and begin the rundown of its old money spinner, Dagenham. With Leyland weakened and unable to rise to volume production, the only alternative is Japanese 'super-screwdriver' operations such as Nissan or Toyota. As cars went, so did tyres, components, associated engineering and electrical industries. Engineering, machine tools, electronics, computers, information technology, carpets and textiles, white goods – all were embarked, to a greater or lesser degree, on the same slope, and not even service industries, banking or financial services were immune.

Facilis descensus Averni. Thatcherites saw Britain as pioneering the way to an interdependent, open, world economy, but the world was hardly like that. Nor was Britain. This was decline into irrelevance: Britain became unable to support itself, influenced and occasionally controlled from outside, a dependent market supplied from outside. That means relegation to a poor periphery, the current state of the North *vis à vis* the South, but inflicted on the whole nation.

An increasing proportion of firms are owned by foreign or multinational companies and ultimately serve interests other than Britain's. A national economy, supplying the world and providing for its own people is becoming a branch economy. Its internationally traded sector, always smaller and weaker, is more so. The country is ceasing to be an export base. The economy is less and less national, more and more supplied, even controlled, from outside. That prospect points to a nation with the research, the design, the training, the skills, the decisions and, thus, the brains taken out – a lobotomized economy. Nations that have wasted their strength, thrown away the tools of management, lost their domestic markets and given up trying, cease to be forces to be reckoned with. He who cannot stay ahead is trampled, becoming dependent. As the industrial base of nationhood is weakened, the structures erected on it begin to lean and topple – towards Europe.

Beggars can't be choosers; neither can dependers be deciders or overflow production facilities head offices. Without national champions, Britain is supplied by other nations and unable to breed its own Euro-champions. Its firms are absorbed into European operations and its market, once rich, becomes a low-return, low-purchasing-power market, demand reduced by unemployment, poverty and the squeeze to balance payments. Capital flows compound the process of peripheralization as we export capital for portfolio or long-term investment, to take over companies and diversify, but import it either as a high-interest entrepôt for funny money, or in the form of take-overs to establish British distribution facilities, and integrate British firms into Continental operations to serve our market but not necessarily our interests. We are vulnerable because we are more open. The government declines to interfere on the grounds that, for British capitalism to be free to take firms in the US, European and Japanese capitalism has to have the same freedom here more dependent on capital inflows to close the horrendous payments gap. This, and the seedcorn guzzle of the 1980s, guarantee lower living standards later as we pay back the borrowing, make good the ground.

Britain has less control over its own economy than its competitors do. A higher proportion of its domestic market is taken by imports. More of its capacity is devoted to assembly, distribution or serving imports. More of its firms are multi-nationals or controlled from outside, ultimately committed to purposes other than ours. The world may be kind. It may not. A nation without an independent, self-sustaining economic base will find out. It cannot float on oil for ever, and as the wells dry, head offices elsewhere, more concerned with their interests than ours, are more likely to close, or contract, peripheral facilities in the hard times.

Having grown to strength by building up powerful industries and national champions, living by exports and taking on the world, competing economies have liberalized from a position of strength: taking in more imports, opening up markets, all without damage to the strong national base. For us, openness without strength was decline, for the base could not face the exposure and the market cried out to be supplied by more dynamic and bigger-scale industry elsewhere. In Britain, production for Europe must be loaded on vessels. Only that marginal part of European manufacture destined for Britain carries such extra costs. Our production is less efficient with a less skilled and educated workforce in industries that have neither invested in robots for flexible batch production, nor grown to take advantage of economies of scale. Productivity below international levels is not compensated by a competitive currency but made worse by the tribute of high interest rates that finance takes to make up for the national failure to grow. We are making our own bed and will eventually all have to lie on it. This process of de-nationalizing or un-nationhood is irreversible.

Round 3 of Maggie versus the 20th century leaves us no longer a world leader with national champions but a branch economy, pulled from outside, its destinies decided there. That trend has hardened for two decades during which 1 million jobs have been lost to Europe, 3 million from industry, and a rising proportion of our demand has been filled from beyond our borders. Britain's share of footloose multinational investment has declined but we have become more dependent on it. All these trends will get worse. The Golden Triangle becoming more attractive, Britain less, as deflation bites and oil fades. The Channel Tunnel will make it easier to supply the periphery from the centre. The Single Market will remove remaining protective barriers for finance, public contracting and defence. European firms have every incentive to set up ancillaries here or take over British ones to mop up the British market, not to use Britain as a productive base from which to export.

Not disaster. Just irrelevance. A C2 nation slipping to D. The British market will get poorer; the Lawson deflation is a taste of what is to come. The industrial engine is losing power. That means becoming an industrial colony of West Germany, pulled by Europe, not pulling it. Oil provided a temporary boost, but it is now petering out. Finance was the chosen alternative, but its contribution in jobs is small, and that, and its share of world financial trade, are both declining because it depends ultimately on industry's ability to generate the wealth for it to manipulate round the world. It also faces intensifying competition from more powerful financial sectors that rest on the surpluses generated by successful industrial bases. The financial world will become Japanese as surely as the industrial. Services provide more jobs, though at lower pay, but ultimately they too depend on the wealth, jobs, spending and demand for services of the industrial sector. A high-skill, high-pay, high-demand economy can only grow from powerful industry. As that declines, so must everything else.

Relegation is not comfortable. Not absolute poverty, for the West German industrial engine will drag us behind, but the steady impoverishment that distorts society and perverts politics. Britain was once easy going and charming. Those whom the gods would disappoint they first make charming, but those whom they would destroy they make mad. Our economic management has been, and the decline it leads to will turn charm into bitterness and division, making politics sour, the media nasty and shoddy. Wealth will be comfortable. It can insulate itself in ghettos as it does even in South America, though as the zero-sum society becomes zero-zero, even money might find the world a less pleasant place and risks being bruised, robbed and further segregated. For the rest, the haves will be increasingly threatened by a growing sub-class that cannot be ghettoized for ever, a divided, self-seeking, embittered ghetto in what could be called the Rottweiler society, were it not better described as Fascism. Thatcherism is the first taste. Already the downmarket government of a downmarket nation will neither consult nor listen because it is a government of will. Obstacles are steamrollered, opposition viewed as disloyal, critics condemned to internal exile, bad news suppressed. So what happens when things get worse and stern imperatives take over? The Man on the White Horse then becomes more attractive than democratic alternatives. We know the world to come. We live in a mild version of it.

Britain started its 1000-year story of nationhood as an irrelevant, offshore island; small in population, exporting minerals and raw materials to be worked up elsewhere; a violent, troublesome periphery to a more civilized Europe. In the 16th and 17th centuries, the British were the barbarous isles: a warring, offshore nuisance, sceptred only by empire and industrialization, the one sustaining the other. They transformed Britain into the most powerful and wealthiest part of Europe. Retirement from both great adventures has already gone a long way. It can still be checked. Britain's problem is whether it can be.

Our sense of superiority is fading, becoming more brittle and defiant as we become poor. We can no longer play Greece to the world's new Romans, because we have failed. No one owes us a living just because we once fought to make the world fit for British cars to break down in. The world is a competitive place. Failures are trampled. No charitable foundation allows them an impoverished dignity, for whoever is left behind sinks. So in our decline, we are left with a large population we cannot provide for. It grew with industry and cannot live without it – unless the EC develops a Common People Policy.

Decline leads to a plangent, poor periphery, one that exports remaining skills, wealth and ability to the richer whole, a poor market for their surplus production, a cheap labour facility adding little value to work too unskilled, unimportant or dirty for them to do themselves, an extractive quarry and a dumping ground for the wastes that powerful economies produce and which poor ones must be grateful to receive. Irrelevant islands with a divided, embittered society, offering only a rundown Ruritania: a theme park that preserves a history that does not interest the rest because, unlike theirs, it has ended in failure.

Britain, which once led the way to a better world and whose people still want it, will be relegated to the position of Europe's poor relation. The first industrial nation to emerge, the first to fail, the first to go, because the reverse of *Vorsprung durch Technik* is *Neidergang durch Ufähigkeit*. Not clogs to slippers in three generations but decline from Chamberlain's Weary Titan to Thatcher's Resentful Redundant, limping behind the world, shouting a mixture of defiance, advice and pleas as our competitors leave the irrelevant nation behind.

Appendix 1
Potential Impact Seats

Rank	Seat	*Con/Democrat Marginals* Maj	3rd Vote
1	Portsmouth S	0.4%	7,047
2	Stockton S	1.3%	18,600
3	Cambridge NE	2.5%	4,891
4	Edinburgh W	2.5%	10,957
5	Bath	2.7%	5,507
6	Hereford	2.7%	4,051
7	Colne Valley	3.0%	16,353
8	Hazel Grove	3.4%	6,354
9	Richmond & Barnes	3.9%	3,227
10	Kincardine & Deeside	4.3%	7,624
11	Conwy	7.4%	9,049
12	Cheltenham	7.8%	4,701
13	Plymouth, Sutton	7.9%	8,310
14	Plymouth, Drake	8.0%	9,451
15	Devon N	8.1%	3,467
16	Isle of Wight	8.2%	4,626
17	Oxford W & Abingdon	9.0%	8,108
18	Falmouth & Cambourne	9.3%	11,271
19	Cambridge	9.7%	15,319
20	Stevenage	9.5%	19,229
21	Cornwall N	9.8%	3,719
22	Leeds NW	10.1%	11,210
23	Crosby	10.2%	11,992
24	Devon W & Torridge	11.0%	4,990
25	Chelmsford	11.4%	4,642
26	Pudsey	11.5%	11,461
27	Cornwall SE	11.8%	4,847
28	Littleborough & Saddleworth	12.1%	13,219
29	Eastwood	12.2%	12,305
30	Winchester	12.2%	4,028
Total of Majorities			125,000
Total 3rd Party (Lab) Vote			256,000

Rank	Seat	Maj	3rd vote
	Con/Lab Marginals		
44	Bolton W	8.2%	10,936
45	Bristol E	8.2%	10,247
46	Edinburgh Pentlands	8.3%	11,072
47	Lewisham W	8.3%	7,247
48	Rossendale & Darwen	8.3%	9,097
49	Feltham & Heston	9.1%	9,623
50	City of Chester	9.2%	10,262
51	Luton South	9.6%	9,146
52	Elmet	9.8%	8,755
53	Croydon NW	10.0%	6,363
54	Pembroke	10.0%	14,832
55	Calder Valley	10.2%	13,761
56	Nuneaton	10.3%	10,550
57	Keighley	10.7%	10,041
58	Harlow	10.7%	8,915
59	Ilford S	10.9%	5,928
60	Lewisham E	10.9%	9,118
61	Derby N	11.6%	7,268
62	Dover	11.9%	10,942
63	Bristol NW	12.0%	10,885
64	Vale of Glamorgan	12.1%	8,633
65	Southampton, Itchen	12.2%	13,006
66	Bury N	12.3%	6,804
67	Southampton, Test	12.3%	11,950
68	Lincoln	12.8%	11,319
69	Mitcham & Morden	12.9%	7,930
70	Chorley	13.3%	9,706
71	Leicester NW	13.4%	10,034
72	Hayes & Harlington	13.7%	6,641
73	South Ribble	14.1%	11,746

Total of Majorities	175,000
Total of 3rd Party (All) Vote	293,000
Total of Majorities less 4% swing	47,000
One fifth of 3rd Vote	58,000